knit the sky

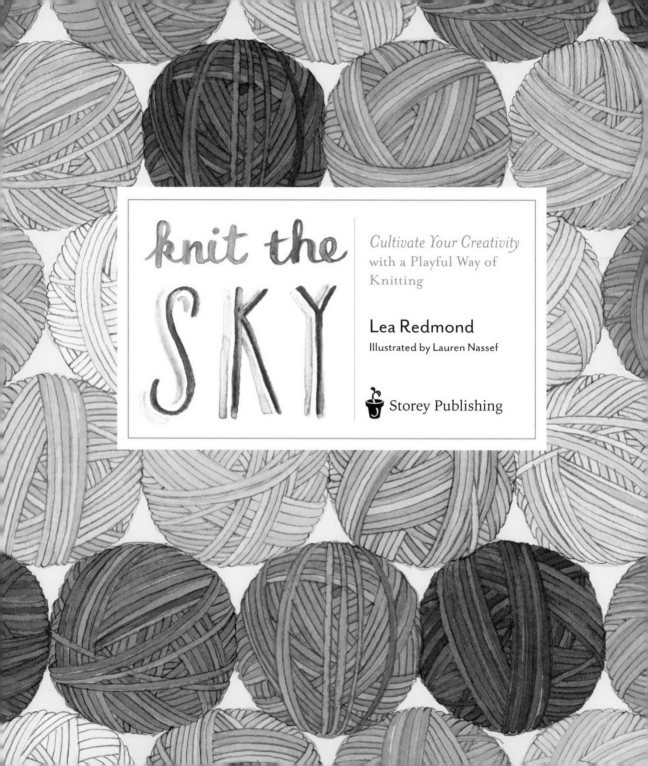

knit the SKY

Cultivate Your Creativity
with a Playful Way of
Knitting

Lea Redmond

Illustrated by Lauren Nassef

Storey Publishing

*The mission of Storey Publishing is to serve our customers by
publishing practical information that encourages
personal independence in harmony with the environment.*

Edited by Gwen Steege
Art direction and book design by Alethea Morrison
Text production by Jennifer Jepson Smith

Cover and interior illustrations by © Lauren Nassef, except for Alison Kolesar, how-to
    illustrations; Ilona Sherratt, charts and diagrams; © Wylius/iStockphoto.com, endsheets
Hand lettering by Alethea Morrison
Indexed by Nancy D. Wood

© 2015 by Lea Redmond

Storey Publishing
210 MASS MoCA Way
North Adams, MA 01247
www.storey.com

Printed in China by R.R. Donnelley
10 9 8 7 6 5 4 3 2 1

LIBRARY OF CONGRESS CATALOGING-IN-PUBLICATION DATA
Redmond, Lea.
 Knit the sky : cultivate your creativity with a playful way of knitting / Lea Redmond.
    pages cm
 ISBN 978-1-61212-333-2 (hardcover : alk. paper)
 ISBN 978-1-61212-334-9 (ebook) 1. Knitting—Patterns. 2. Knitting—Psychological aspects. I. Title.
TT820.R395 2015
746.43'2—dc23
                                                                    2015010745

dedicated to

Ginger, Mary Ann, and Harriet —

three generations of knitters that

came before me

you're invited

Imagine yourself strolling through a park. It is a lovely day, so you kick off your shoes and lie down in the green grass. Folding your arms behind your head, you cloud-gaze for a few minutes — a whale, a harp, a pie. You drift off into a light sleep. The next thing you know, you awake to a raindrop on your cheek. A pack of gray clouds has blown in from the west, and it is starting to sprinkle. You lie on the ground for just a minute more because a gorgeous sliver of sunshine is slipping through the clouds. Then you hop up and run for cover, perhaps to the café across the street where you can sit by the window with a cup of hot chocolate.

What if we could turn an experience like this into a knitting project, translating that snippet of beauty into little loops of yarn? What if we could *knit the sky?* I often wish I could just reach up into the sky and pull some clouds down into my yarn basket! I'll have to do the next best thing: go to the yarn store and collect skeins in a spectrum of sky colors — blues, grays, and white. Then I'll return to my window and knit with the strands that best match that day's weather. And tomorrow, repeat. Each day will be a chance to pause, look up, and notice the ever-present swirling show above our heads. If I keep at it for 365 days, I will make a one-year weather report in the shape of a scarf!

This book chronicles the many knitting adventures that arose as I began to knit the sky. The projects that follow are knitting patterns, but with a twist. Think of them more like dance partners. As you engage them, they will respond to you, ask things of you, and surprise you.

To complete these knitting projects, you will need to look up from your needles and bring your attention to the world around you. You will draw on your own sense of whimsy and adventure as you infuse your knitting with your life, and vice versa. One project requires that you wake up before dawn. Another asks you to see like a bee. Yet another recalls the delight of splitting a twin-stick Popsicle with a friend. We will seek the marvelous in the mundane as we knit on the subway, watch a baseball game, or skip through piles of leaves. Along the way, we will make things, but we will also make memories. We might even make new friends. Please join me!

This book is a proposal to knitters everywhere, beginners and experts alike. I would like to suggest that we knitters expand the territory of what we consider to be a pattern. It is commonly thought that the pattern begins with casting on and ends with weaving in loose ends. Everything we need to know is there in ink on paper. There is a photo so we can know that we're on the right track. And this is a perfectly wonderful way to knit. I humbly bow to any sweater handstitched with love. Similarly, I stand in awe

of the many stunning garments knitters are making that exhibit technical mastery. If you are reading this book, you likely know the extreme pleasure of gifting something as simple as a handknit hat. These pleasures are at the heart of this book. They are the starting point, the seed, the enduring core. I just want to be sure that *one* way to knit — browsing, choosing, and following predesigned patterns — isn't mistaken for the *one and only* way to knit. Our craft is much bigger than that. It always has been. It is true: stories and meaning have always infused handknit items, such as the joy that permeates any baby blanket, or the memory your very first project carries of the person who taught you to knit. The power of these stories and experiences is part of what keeps us coming back to our needles again and again. In this book, I would like to draw attention to the already storied nature of knitting and to explore ways to creatively engage that phenomenon in a way that deepens our humanity, both as individuals and as social creatures.

Making in this way means giving as much weight to *process* as to *product.* Or, put another way, it means expanding our notion of "product" to include all of the hidden elements wrapped up in the making of a thing. From this perspective, we are never *just* making a hat or a pair of socks; we are always also making a world, our own little world as well as the bigger common world. If we do not focus only on the finished garment, we can stand back and take a wider view. Did you laugh in the middle of a row? Did you run into an old friend on your way to the yarn shop? Did your sister shed a few tears when she received the baby blanket? This world of experience, this field of relations, is what we truly make when we knit. So if we consider the full life of a garment, from the gathering of yarn to the knitting to the way the garment is eventually worn, every step along the way becomes an opportunity for creative play. Each seemingly ephemeral moment is an opportunity to be radically thoughtful and make things count. Since, as it turns out, we are making a whole world, we might as well make it as wonderful as we can.

To be clear, I do not value process *over* aesthetic results; the garments we make should absolutely be beautiful and aesthetically interesting — soft, elegant, warm, patterned. Rather, I want to propose that an essential part of any item's beauty is the activity and meaning it gathers, the weighty wonderfulness that comes with being connected in a broader field. I want to integrate process and product, letting life — moments past, present, and future — find its way into the aesthetic itself, influencing what the finished garment looks like, its colors, textures, shapes. I wish to see garments that embody meaning and tell stories in ways both explicit and implicit. I dream of garments in which the aesthetic qualities are not just objectively beautiful for formal reasons, but also beautiful because they were thoughtfully chosen for particular reasons by particular people who brought the full force of their hearts and minds to the task.

And the party isn't over at bind off. With the expanded notion of making that I like to assume, a garment is never truly done. Yes, we will weave in all the loose ends and make sure it fits, but there is more. The handknit results of the patterns in this book are not only records of past processes. They are not mere silent artifacts left over from adventures come and gone. Quite the contrary. As these items are put to good use, they will take on new lives of their own, continuing to remind, inspire, and connect us with the people, places, and ideas we care about. All those future possibilities are part of what the garment *is*, and what it *can be*. Despite how all this might sound, this way of knitting — this way of being — need not be overly complicated. It certainly is not abstract. Just like dancing, the best way to learn the steps is to do them and develop intuition for them. So, welcome!

Given the unusual nature of the projects in this book, its format might be a bit surprising, too. For one thing, there is not a single photograph of a finished project. This is because the look of the final garments is yet to be determined — by you — and the ones you make will be wonderfully different from the ones other knitters make or the ones I have made. Each of us is a unique individual, and the final aesthetic of our pieces will reflect that fact. Some of the patterns call for particular colors and weights of yarn, but many of them are open-ended. A few of them don't even suggest a particular type of garment to knit: you get to choose a favorite pattern from elsewhere and let it give shape to the concepts described in this book's patterns. When a particular technique is required, such as carrying multiple strands up the edge of a scarf, or when a specific stitch is recommended, such as the Raspberry Stitch, you'll find basic instructions in the appendix, but there is always a lot of leeway for you to explore your own ideas. This incompleteness is intentional. It is to give you the space to make these projects truly your own, to decide for yourself what is most fitting. There is even a brief section near the end that guides you to invent your own patterns in the spirit of this book. I have tried to provide everything you need to begin, and the rest is up to you.

My hope is that this book sends you out into the world and deep within your heart, knitting along the way. Each project is an invitation to explore and engage, to be observant and contemplative, loving and patient, bold and playful. If you fall in love with this way of knitting, it is first and foremost because you are in love with life. Whether you are a beginner or an advanced knitter, you already have the most important thing you need to be good at this way of knitting: a human heart. My hope is that my musings inspire you not only to do some of these projects and also to put your own spin on them, but to invent your own projects from scratch. Please feel free to adjust any of my instructions so they feel right for you. Swap in a different garment type. Make the blanket bigger. Change the colors. This book is an experiment in thinking as much as it is a book of patterns to actually make. It is inevitably a reflection of me and my particular interests, passions, and memories. It is what arises when *my* heart meets *my* knitting needles at *this* moment in my life. I invite you to make any of my projects that speak to you, and I encourage you to also make up your own. When you truly let your heart meet your own set of needles, what might you make?

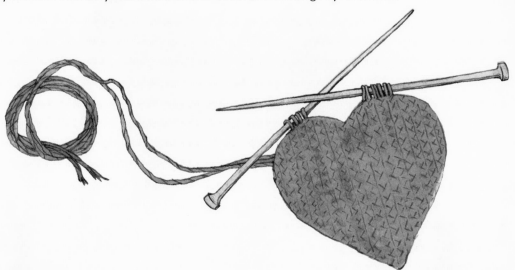

knit the SKY

WHEN WAS THE LAST TIME you lay on the grass and watched the clouds drift by? Can you recall whether the sky was a brilliant blue or a hazy shade of gray yesterday? What about the day before? And the one before that? Did you take the time to notice? It's surprisingly easy to forget to look up and appreciate the colorful show that swirls above our heads at every moment. This project asks you to keep an eye on the weather and to track its comings and goings more closely than usual.

Each day, you will knit a stripe in colors that match that particular day's sky, slowly creating your own wearable weather report.

As your daily observations meet the clicking of your needles, nature's patterns — both predictable and erratic — will emerge as the days pile up. Just like the weather, your scarf design will largely be out of your control. You are likely to be surprised by delightful sequences of alternating colors that you never would have devised on your own. Winter's whites and grays might tire you. But as you heed nature's ways, you might also learn something about the beauty of waiting. Is a bright blue sky lovelier if you've knit a month of gray stripes in anticipation? Is a gray stripe more meaningful if you remember getting caught in a sudden storm with a friend and no umbrella?

With each sunset, the colors of an unrepeatable day fade into the night. Unlike knitting, we can't unravel a day and relive it. But as the days slip through our fingers, so does our yarn. At the end of a year, you will have

Oakland

Santa Fe

Copenhagen

Seattle

a scarf that the clouds have drifted through. Bind off, keep warm, and let your beautiful garment remind you to keep looking up.

Prepare Your Palette

First, gather balls of laceweight yarn that correspond to the various colors of the daytime sky: bright blue, light blue, white, light gray, and dark gray. Using laceweight yarns means you can use the strands doubled so that you have more color options for illustrating the sky. Using US 3 needles, you'll get a gauge of about 7 stitches to an inch. For example, on a partly cloudy day you might select white and light blue. For a thunderstorm, you might combine light gray and dark gray. And for a pure bright blue sky, you might choose to knit the stripe with two bright blue strands. Make two separate balls of some colors so you'll have the option for the latter. I've found that it's usually sufficient to split only the two blues (the bright and the light blues) in half. Virtually all weather conditions can be represented by creative pairings of the resulting seven balls of yarn.

Check the Weather

Begin your scarf by choosing the two-strand color combination that best represents the weather on the first day of your project. Treating these two strands as one, cast on 40 stitches. Then, day after day, observe the sky, select the two colors that express its essence best, and add a stripe to your scarf by working 2 rows in garter stitch with those yarns. Continue for a year. Bind off and weave in loose ends.

For advice on how to handle a large number of yarns as you work, see page 141.

At What Hour?

You might want to observe the sky at the same time each day. Or you might want to wait until each evening and reflect on the essence of that day's weather as a whole. For example, even if a bright blue sky prevailed for most of the day, you might still choose gray yarns to represent the booming thunderstorm that suddenly swept through town in the afternoon.

If You Forget a Day . . .

- Ask a friend or a neighbor if they can remember what the sky was like that day.
- Check your local weather records.
- Choose an entirely new color (like red or green) to represent the rare day when you forget to notice the sky.

If You're Too Busy . . .

If you're too busy to knit a stripe one day, snap a quick photo of the sky and catch up later!

If You Travel . . .

Since this scarf is your own personal weather report, it's okay to incorporate weather observations from other places as you travel. Take the project with you on the road to stay on schedule. Or leave it at home, but snap photos of the sky and jot down daily notes to help you get caught up upon your return.

Fancy and Festive

- Knit clear glass beads (see page 146) into your scarf on rainy days.
- Begin on New Year's Day, summer solstice, winter solstice, or your birthday.

bundle of JOY

M AKING A STRIPED SCARF is not the only way to knit the sky. We can also take aesthetic inspiration from the layout of a wall calendar in which each day is represented by a small square. Imagine connecting all those pages of days into one big sheet. Ta-da — a blanket! Knitting the sky into a blanket makes a sweet newborn gift, especially since the baby is missing out on all those skies while he or she is in the dark womb. As soon as you learn about the pregnancy of a loved one, gather your yarn in a jiffy and begin knitting a square a day in colors that match the weather. Piece the squares together along the way to keep everything tidy and in the proper order. Continue for the rest of the pregnancy and bind off on the day the baby is born.

This also makes a great project for expectant mommies or daddies to knit while they wait for the birth of their own child.

Knitting the sky into a blanket makes an especially sweet newborn gift.

A (Very) Little Math

To make this project manageable, you need to do a bit of planning before you begin. Of course, you won't know exactly how many squares you're going to be knitting before the baby is born, but imagine that you learn about the event about seven months before the baby is due. You might then estimate that you'll need about 210 squares (7 months × 30 days/month). With 210 squares to work with, your blanket could be 14 squares wide by 15 squares long. If you make 3-inch squares, your blanket will be 42 by 45 inches, which is just about right for a baby! It's unlikely that you'll have happened to complete a row on the baby's birth day, so just knit that last piece wider than all the rest to fill out the row of squares.

Purchase yarn in the colors suggested for knitting the sky scarf (page 14). You can also use the same weight yarns (two strands of laceweight yarns held together with US 3 needles). Cast on enough stitches for 3 inches. You will probably get about 7 stitches to an inch with this weight yarn and this size needles, so cast on 21 stitches. The exact size of the finished blanket isn't critical, but this approach should get you in the ballpark and also result in a fabric that feels nice. Knit until the piece is 3 inches square and then bind off. (You'll find instructions for how to join the squares together on pages 141–143.)

One by One

It's fun to approach this project as if you were making a patchwork quilt. Knit each of the 3-inch squares as a separate unit, and then sew or crochet them together as you complete each one, so that you maintain the order and also so that you aren't faced with stitching together more than 200 squares all at once when it's time to present your gift.

Baby Soft

Babies have infamously soft, delicate skin, so be sure to choose yarn for the blanket that's appropriate for a newborn. I recommend superwash wool or 100% cotton so that it's not only super soft but also machine washable. New parents are unlikely to have a lot of extra time for hand-washing!

Be Playful

If knitting square after square in plain garter stitch (knitting every row) seems boring, these little squares are the perfect chance to try out new stitch patterns. Think of each one as a different facial expression to engage and delight the baby. Find a good stitch dictionary and expand your stitch repertoire! Keep in mind that different stitch patterns result in different gauges, so rather than knitting the same number of rows (and stitches per row) as you would if you were knitting them all in garter stitch, adjust the counts in order to keep the dimensions of all the squares consistent.

SWEET possibilities

"WHAT COLOR GUMBALL DID YOU GET?" As a child, not only did I care remarkably much which color I got, I also wanted to know what color my friend got. Red? Purple? White? I especially wanted to know if my brother got pink. And when I'd insert a coin, twist the knob, and my favorite color — purple — tumbled down the chute just for me, it was my lucky day. The brilliance of a bubble gumball is this: it is both candy and toy, a playful sweet sphere that begins with a coin and a small mystery — what color will I get?

I had my very own gumball machine when I was a child. It was the real deal: a brilliant glass globe filled with a rainbow of gumballs, a shiny red metal base, a coin mechanism with a satisfying click, and a key to eventually reclaim my own quarters. Perhaps surprisingly, being able to open up the machine and cherry-pick my color was not at all tempting. I readily accepted the risk of not getting my favorite color in exchange for the delight of a guaranteed surprise, proof that life can be dull if we always get exactly what we think we want.

This knitting project gives us an excuse to revisit the gumball machines of childhood in the service of a new mission: a pair of colorful striped socks. You will purchase gumballs along the way to determine the sequence of colors in each sock.

The gumball machines of yesteryear are still very much alive and well, and waiting for you just where you left them at age 10. Fill your pockets or purse with quarters, and head out in search of the one nearest you. You might feel a little absurd pocketing ball after ball, but it's worth it. You are a serious knitter, you mean business, and you will go to any length for a genuine pair of gumball socks. You might even blow a bubble or two as you stroll away with your haul.

Choose a Strategy

You can use the basic sock pattern found on pages 147–149 or your own favorite design. Gather together gumball-colored yarns in the appropriate gauge for the sock pattern you've selected. Pink, white, blue, green, orange, red, yellow, and purple are the most common colors you'll see. Turn the skeins into nice tidy balls — gumball shaped, of course! — one for each color.

You can purchase your gumballs one at a time as you stumble upon machines, remembering the color each time so you can add a matching round to your in-process sock. Or you can buy them all at once, being sure to record the order of colors in a notebook as the balls are dispensed. Bring a bag to carry all those gumballs home! Enjoy a chewy mouthful of nostalgia as you knit, making the stripes whatever width you desire and perhaps blowing and popping a big huge bubble at the end of each round.

A Gumball Gift

If you make a pair of gumball socks as a gift, consider filling a glass jar with the gumballs you collect for the project. Tie a ribbon around the jar and give it along with the socks. Or fill the socks themselves with the gumballs and tie them closed at the top!

Mix and Match

Socks almost always come in pairs of two that are identical. Even when we're in a rush in the morning, many of us will tear through a dresser drawer trying to find a match. Gumball socks are a chance to mix things up. Instead of copying the stripe pattern from the first sock to the second, subject the second sock to the same probability scenario as the first. Although the finished socks might appear identical, closer inspection reveals that the color sequences are different. Each sock is just one tangible result of the mind-boggling array of combinatorial possibility hiding inside each gumball machine.

twin-stick TREAT

S NAP! One Popsicle suddenly becomes two: one for me and one for you. The classic frozen treat with two wooden sticks and a deep indentation down the middle is elegant in design and rich in metaphor. Invented during the Great Depression, the creative two-stick Popsicle design preserved the affordability of these frozen treats. For a relatively small increase in the production cost of each Popsicle, the Popsicle company could serve two customers at once, lowering the price per person. As long as a pair of friends or siblings could agree on which flavor to share (not always an easy thing to do!), they could pool their pennies and enjoy a refreshing treat together, perhaps forgetting their financial woes for a few sweet minutes.

To knit in the spirit of a twin-stick Popsicle, you and a friend will knit two scarves at once on one pair of needles.

I recommend sitting side by side with your friend so that you can pass the project back and forth, taking turns adding a number of rows to each scarf when it's your turn to knit. This is a great excuse to get together on a regular basis and catch up over tea. As you share this knitting project, you might also share stories and secrets, fears and dreams. Like the original two-stick Popsicle, this is a one-color project. Choose the yarn together; there is surely at least one color in the local yarn shop that you both love. Two scarves will soon take shape upon one set of needles. When the scarves are the length you want, cast each of them off to "break" this twin-stick Popsicle in half: one scarf for you and one scarf for your friend. Continue to share the experience for years to come as you wear your twin scarves again and again. Unlike the original Popsicle, of course, these scarves are better enjoyed in winter than summer. (For advice about stitch counts and standard scarf lengths and widths, see pages 163–164.)

How It's Done

Knitting two scarves at once on one set of needles is, I promise, much simpler than it sounds. You simply use two balls of yarn, one for each scarf, and take care to switch yarns each time you transition from one scarf to the next. Choose a set of straight needles long enough to accommodate two scarves, or use a circular needle if you prefer.

1. Using one of the balls of yarn, cast on stitches for scarf #1. Take the second ball of yarn and cast on stitches for scarf #2 on the same needle, right next to the stitches for #1. Turn your needle around to get ready to knit.

2. Knit a row on scarf #2 with the second ball of yarn. When you get to the end of this row on scarf #2, you'll find that the yarn for scarf #1 is waiting for you right across from it. Drop the yarn for scarf #2 and pick up the scarf #1 yarn (take care not to twist the yarns around each other), and knit across scarf #1 to the end of the row. Turn your needle.

3. Knit back across scarf #1 with that same ball, then switch to the second ball of yarn (which is waiting for you) and knit across scarf #2. Turn your needle.

Repeat steps 2 and 3 for several rows, then pass the needles to your friend so she can take a turn adding to the pair of scarves in the same way.

Add Your Signature

It adds a subtle layer of interest to the finished scarves if each knitter chooses her own signature stitch pattern and sticks to it on her turns. For example, one friend could always knit in garter stitch (knit every row), while the other friend always knits in Seed Stitch (K1, P1 across, then purl the knit stitches and knit the purl stitches on the way back). Since the final scarves are solid in color, they will appear to be the same from afar. But up close, you can enjoy knowing which rows were laid down by each knitter based on the alternating sections of decorative texture.

Sharing: Random or Planned?

How do you know when it's time to pass the project back and forth? It's up to you. As a team, decide how to best approach the logistics. If you live near each other, you can just get together whenever it's convenient and each add a few inches to the project while you visit. Or you can make this a long-distance project with a friend in another town, mailing the in-process scarf back and forth to take turns. You can each add a specific length before switching off, resulting in even repeats of the surface texture. Or you can play it by ear and simply send it back and forth whenever the inspiration strikes or it's most convenient. The resulting aesthetic will be less orderly, but perhaps more true to the spontaneous pattern of most daily lives.

mood RING

KNITTING HAS ALWAYS BEEN A REFUGE FOR ME. A project, tucked in my purse or resting on my armchair, is like having my own little retreat center at my fingertips. Whenever I have a big decision to make, have complex emotions to work through, or simply need to take some deep breaths, I pick up my knitting and am instantly transported to another realm.

In a way, the steady stream of emotions and thoughts that transpire as I'm knitting always makes its way into the garment. With most projects, these ethereal details end up lost forever. But with this project, multiple colors will represent our feelings, recording the ups and downs of our daily emotional lives and making the invisible visible. Over time, a bird's-eye view will emerge, and the course of our moods will begin to reveal itself. At its best, this will empower us to be proactive about our emotional health. If we keep knitting along the way, our soft, fuzzy feedback loops will let us know how often we are melancholy or contented.

This project, a colorful cowl that tracks your mood for one month and fits nicely around your neck, is a knit version of a mood ring.

Do you remember mood rings? They claim to hold magic stones that change color with our moods. While I am not at all convinced that they actually work, they are certainly a lovely idea. How convenient to have a ring on your finger that keeps tabs on your emotional state at all times, even when you are unable to see yourself clearly. As your knit version of a mood ring grows to reveal your inner life, you will gain a similar clarity. You can even make subtle adjustments to your daily routine along the way. Call a friend or take a different route home from work. Mix things up and the effects might surface in future rows.

Keep in mind that the human heart is complex, and monitoring one's mood is not an exact science. You may not be able to control enough factors to know if a particular change led to a particular result. Nevertheless, it's likely that you can glean some sort of meaning from the simple practice of paying close attention. While I wish you much orange (happiness) and yellow (calm), we should not assume that this is necessarily the goal of this project. Disappointment, frustration, and restlessness are often inevitable side effects of a diligent search for fulfillment, whether it's personal or professional. It really is up to you to decide what kind of emotional rainbow is healthy and satisfying for you. Blue stripes (sadness) can be beautiful, too.

A Ring That Fits You

Choose any cowl pattern that strikes your fancy, or use the one on page 155 for a simple ribbed cowl. If you are using your own pattern, it should have at least 150 rows, letting you add 5 rows per day for an entire month. Collect colorful yarns that are all the same weight. Emotions are complex and can change quickly. Adding 5 or more rows per day will let you use multiple colors for each day, more accurately capturing the emotional nuances of your days. If one day contains both joyful moments and sad moments, knit both of those colors into your cowl, as separate rows in the order in which the emotions took place.

Color Code

As you knit your "mood ring," you can use the color meanings I provide in the key on the opposite page or devise your own. Also, if there is a particular emotion or mood you want to track closely, your whole project can revolve around it. For example, if your biggest concern is stress, the meaning of your color spectrum could range from very stressful (red) to very calm (blue).

Sock Set, Data Set

If you want to track your mood for an entire year instead of just one month, maybe you'd like to knit a dozen socks (six pairs). After you knit each sock, embroider the name of the month onto the toe. (Use just a strand or two of embroidery thread so it doesn't create an uncomfortable lump in your shoes!) After one year, lay them out in the order of the months for a bigger data set and enhanced perspective. Mix and match when you wear them.

Blue

sad, fearful, disappointed, exhausted, heartbroken, unappreciated, restless, unable to let go, shameful, hesitant

black

powerful, secretive, fancy, lonely, lost, depressed, disoriented, formal, defeated

green

bored, cautious, awkward, indecisive, vulnerable, tired, restless, neutral, in limbo, passive

yellow

content, safe, relaxed, cheerful, compassionate, even-keeled, calm, mellow, satisfied, nostalgic, peaceful

white

open-minded, aware, trusting, magnanimous, serene, meditative, tranquil, infinite

orange

joyful, inspired, creative, playful, optimistic, spontaneous, motivated, productive, hopeful, lucky, eager

red

thrilled, passionate, courageous, surprised, romantic, adventurous, elated, radiant, enthusiastic, excited

Brown

rooted, connected, centered, balanced, whole, secure, natural, earthy

purple

angry, anxious, scared, stressed, confused, envious, nervous, irritated, flustered, frustrated, hurt, regretful

NECTAR collector

LIKE KNITTERS, BEES LOVE PATTERNS. The repeating hexagonal structure of their honeycomb is both practical and stunning. Like my favorite pair of socks, bees' bodies feature bright stripes. Bees even dance, communicating with each other by way of tiny figure eights in the air. Although scientists have discovered that the six-sided walls of the honeycomb allow for maximum efficiency of material and labor, they are less certain than they once were about the purpose of the "waggle" dances. In some habitats, honeybee dancing seems to stimulate foraging, while in others it appears superfluous, an extravagance I'm delighted to know about. I like the idea that evolution simply loves to shake it!

Here's your assignment: stick your nose deep into flowers, inhale, and knit a honeycomb purse.

I invite you to join me in a flight of fancy. Let's pretend we're bees for a bit and knit along the way. If nothing is blooming where you live right now, you'll need to wait for spring to begin this project, just like a bee huddled in its hive keeping warm. But when the first blooms of spring appear, hurry to the yarn shop. You'll need enough yarn to make a big handful of hexagons, one at a time, filling each one with honey-colored stitches and piecing them together into a purse.

Rules of the Game

Worker bees work their little tails off; a quart of honey might contain 48,000 miles worth of nectar-gathering flight. That is equal to almost two laps around the world! As such, let's outline a few rules to ensure this project isn't too easy.

- After smelling one or more flowers during a particular outing, you can knit just one corresponding hexagon. You cannot simply smell a bunch of flowers all at once and then knit the whole purse in one go. No fragrance hoarding allowed! Bees must make many trips back and forth between flowers and the hive. So shall you!

- Considering that a colony of bees typically stays within two miles of its hive, you can only knit a hexagon if its corresponding flower grows within two miles of your home. You might want to print out a map, draw a circle with a two-mile radius around your home, and keep it in your pocket. Since you cannot fly, and since bees don't have cars or bicycles, you must go on foot. Take a water bottle if necessary.

- Red flowers are off-limits and do not count. Honeybees cannot see the color red, and for our purposes here, neither can you!

Getting Down to Bees-ness

Linen yarn is a good choice for this purse because it is strong and not too stretchy. We don't want any lip balm slipping through! Linen is also a poetically good choice because it is a plant-based yarn that started its life among beautiful blue flax flowers. Find two colors of linen yarn: a honey-inspired golden and a wax-inspired yellow. You'll use yellow for the cast on and one row of edging, then switch to the golden yarn to knit to the center of each hexagon. Using size US 5 double-pointed needles, follow the stitch pattern on page 152, making 24 hexagons for the purse pattern on page 154. Depending on the look you like best, use mattress stitch or crochet to join the shapes (pages 141–142).

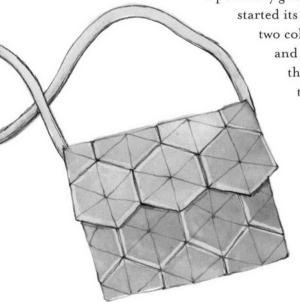

A Smaller Sip

If piecing together all those hexagons sounds tedious to you, make a set of hexagon-shaped coasters instead. A set of four coasters is a great little project and makes an especially lovely housewarming gift. For coasters, cast on a few more stitches than suggested for the purse's hexagons, so the resulting hexagons are standard coaster size (see page 153).

Shake It!

After you have finished your handknit honeycomb purse (and possibly pollinated some flowers with your nose), swing it over your shoulder and let it remind you to enjoy simple pleasures like the flowers in your neighborhood. Your local honeybees are surely focused on the precise locations of the sweetest flowers, but we humans sometimes forget they're even there. And don't be surprised if your new purse inspires your very own extravagantly superfluous waggle dance.

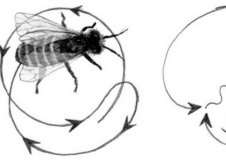 

Host a Knitting Bee

Bees are social creatures, and so are we. If you and a group of friends are looking for a gift for someone special whom you all know and love, you could all smell flowers and knit hexagons. When, all added together, you have 24 hexagons ready, get together to connect them into the finished purse for your mutual friend.

patchwork POSTCARDS

WHETHER TRAVERSING FOREIGN LANDS or taking a road trip closer to home, I love to chronicle the natural and cultural contours of my adventures. Some travelers keep diaries and sketchbooks. Others keep cameras around their necks. Still others write postcards to friends and family back home. What is a knitter to do, especially when packing light?

Here's my suggestion: Instead of picking through postcard racks, seek out local yarn shops and sort through skeins. Collect colors of yarn that remind you of the places you are exploring.

As you travel, knit postcard-size swatches along the way and send them home one at a time — addressed to yourself!

Especially if you are traveling abroad, your visit to each post office itself might become an adventure as you navigate language barriers and unfamiliar postal systems. Be sure to ask to see the various postage stamps available to choose from and to have your little parcel weighed for the proper amount of postage. And don't forget to notice the diversity of post boxes from place to place as you slip envelopes stuffed with swatches through the mail slots. (If you have extra yarn when you leave a place and want to keep it without having to carry it, just mail it home as well.)

Up, Up, and Away!
Pigeon post aside, the first airmail parcels were delivered across international borders in the late 1700s by hot air balloons. May your own colorful swatches fly through the air in the same adventurous spirit!

A Colorful Experience

Here are a few examples of what it might mean to choose colors based on places and experiences. If you like, write a few notes on each envelope to help you remember why you chose each particular color.

· Cobalt blue for a Chinese porcelain exhibit you saw in Beijing
· Red-orange for the sandstone of Arches National Park in Utah
· Blue-gray for a foggy visit to the seaside of Massachusetts
· Bright green for the moss-covered trees of the Oregon coast
· Red for a favorite strawberry tart in Paris
· Light green for all the green tea you drank in Japan
· A rainbow of colors inspired by the Festival of Colors in India
· Deep midnight blue for a canoe trip on the Boundary Waters
· Orange for the single starfish you saw in the tide pools of Northern California

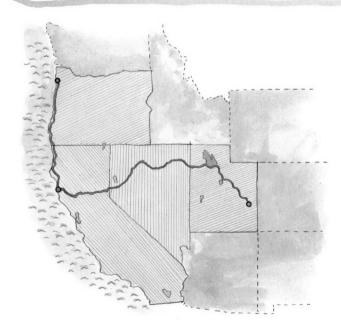

Special Delivery

Upon your return home, you will find a big, puffy pile of mail waiting for reminiscing. Pull each swatch out of its envelope and remember the sensory details of your trip. Then, piece them all together to make something as small as a scarf or as large as a throw. Or save up knit postcards from many trips and then piece them all together into a single travel record. If you like, you can use the dates of the postmarks on the envelopes as an organizing principle for your piecing process, attaching the swatches to each other in the same order in which you traveled to each place.

What's on the Needles

Postcards are typically 4 by 6 inches or 5 by 7 inches, so those are good sizes for your handknit ones, too. They will be much easier to piece together later on if you choose one size and stick to it for all of them. As long as you are okay with variations in thickness in the final garment, you may use various needle sizes and yarn gauges for the swatches. It will make it easier to piece them together if you leave a couple of feet of yarn at the end when you bind off. You can use that for seaming and avoid weaving in two additional ends. (For advice on how to join the pieces once you're home, see pages 141–143.)

Postal Borders

After all the pieces are stitched together, you might want to finish off the postal theme by adding a white border around the entire piece, like the one on a vintage postcard or a postage stamp. With white yarn and a long circular needle, pick up stitches on all four sides, and then knit several rounds of garter stitch until you have a border that's the right scale for your scarf or throw. (For how to pick up stitches, see page 144.) *Important:* Be sure to increase 1 stitch on both sides of each corner stitch in every round so that the border lies flat and doesn't curl up at the corners. For a true postage-stamp effect, you could use a Picot Bind Off to create a perforated edge all the way around. (See page 144 for Picot Bind Off.)

Create a Memory Journal

After emptying your envelopes, turn them into a keepsake journal by binding them into a book. This is especially fun if you have written notes about the colors and places on the backs of the envelopes. You can even put a length of the corresponding yarns inside the envelopes and refer to the book in the future as a key to decode the meaning of your final scarf or throw. If you know you want to do this, be sure to keep a piece of each yarn along the way.

Other Itineraries

- Choose yarn along the way and ship whole skeins home without knitting them during your trip. When you get home, you can combine all your skeins into a project.
- Make this a group project: Instead of just sending the "postcards" to yourself, send them to knitter friends whenever you travel. Each of you then constructs an item from both your own and your friends' handknit postcards.

Be Prepared

Since it might be difficult to find envelopes along the way, carry a roll of tape with you and make your own envelopes by simply folding any thick paper material around your swatch and taping it around all the edges. Or, if you can fit them in your suitcase, travel with a stack of official blue-and-red-striped airmail envelopes.

doodle DAYDREAM

As a young student, did you fill in circles on standardized test forms with a number 2 pencil? Well, this project is the opposite of that seminal school-age experience. Instead of constraining ourselves to tight spaces and right (or wrong) answers, we'll be doodling away in the margins and losing track of time. We will, however, still use pencils, for the sake of nostalgia and just plain fun. That's right; we'll be knitting using pencils instead of needles. Just like in school, if you don't have a couple of pencils handy, you might have to tap a neighbor on the shoulder and ask if you can borrow some. Then pretend that class has started, but your teacher is dreadfully boring. Instead of throwing paper airplanes or passing notes (you don't want to get in trouble), you'll fill the metaphorical margins of your notebook with a trail of loops upon loops.

We're knitting a pencil skirt on pencil needles in pencil-colored yarns.

Since pencils are shorter than standard knitting needles and can't hold as many stitches, this skirt is constructed with six separate panels. This narrowness gives many opportunities to experiment, or doodle. Here's your chance to try out a series of stitch patterns you may have been curious about: Diagonal Scallop, Seeded Rib (see page 137), Star Cluster, Reverse Stockinette Chevron. Or you can improvise your own on the spot. Either way, give yourself permission to play. Be lighthearted. Do not plan out the sequence of stitch patterns for the panels ahead of time. Just play it by ear: an inch of this, 4 inches of that, a row of this, 2 rows of that. If you pretend there's no purpose and that mistakes are impossible — just like doodling on paper — your final result will actually

be richer. You might get a few inches of patterning that you find dull, but intuition and good luck might also bring you doodles that are delightful beyond expectation. As you knit, if something emerges that you honestly just can't stand, use your "eraser" and pull out a few stitches (or rows). But try to use this eraser sparingly; pretend it is small, like the one on your pencil.

Get Your Pencils and Paper Ready!

After finding a pair of pencils, give them a good sharpening. Scribble on paper to dull the points a little so they don't poke you while you're knitting. You can also smooth the pencil tips with sandpaper if the pencil sharpener doesn't leave a smooth surface. This will keep your yarn from snagging on the exposed wood. A great way to keep stitches from falling off the ends of the pencils is to put pink cap erasers on their ends.

For yarn, I recommend knitting with two strands at once — with two different shades of gray — to add interest and complexity. It will be as if one of your pencil needles contains a light gray lead and the other a darker one, each leaving a loopy graphite trail behind it. Standard pencils are about the width of size US 11 knitting needles, so use yarn intended for size US 5 or 6 needles so that you can double up the strands and obtain the proper gauge when you use the pencils. Your final gauge will be around 3½ to 4 stitches per inch, resulting in a nice thick winter skirt, perfect for wearing with leggings. (For pencil skirt knitting instructions, see page 162.)

Extra Credit

- If cables are part of your doodling, you can easily make a cable needle out of a third pencil. Simply break the pencil in half and sharpen both ends. Dull and sand as needed. Voilà!
- Keep in mind that some pattern stitches create a fabric that is less stretchy than others. Be careful not to use too many stitches that pull the yarn tightly, as that might affect the size of your final skirt. You might, however, want to purposely use tighter pattern stitches in the top section of your skirt near the waist in order to bring in the shape above the hips.
- Remember that a purl stitch will create a bump on the side facing you and a knit stitch will leave a bump on the side facing away from you. This is because knitting and purling are essentially the same stitch, just flipped. You can use this understanding to improvise your own pattern stitches.

MONSTER
under your bed

As a child, were you afraid of the dark? Did monsters creep about your bedroom as you tried to fall asleep? I was protected by a night-light in the form of a little ceramic house, given to me by my grandmother. The house had a handful of tiny windows, each glowing with warm yellow light. Only now does it finally occur to me that my parents must have snuck into my room countless times to turn off the lights in the little house after I fell asleep. Some of the monsters lurking in the dark fade away as we grow up. Unfortunately, anxious nights full of tossing and turning still persist for many of us. It turns out that

as adults, we often tussle with bigger and scarier monsters than children do. It's a good thing we had practice as children and built up some tolerance for it.

What is a knitter to do when she wakes up in the middle of the night and can't get back to sleep? I suggest keeping a friendly monster under your bed.

My new cure for insomnia is to keep an in-process knitting project handy that I can reach without getting out of bed. You, too, can keep a friendly monster under your bed, stitching in the dark to calm yourself back to sleep. And if you truly can't sleep, at least you'll make something! You can also add to your friendly monster a little bit each night before you even try to fall asleep, as a pleasant preparation for sweet dreams. A throw project makes a perfect friendly monster. As it grows, it will keep you extra cozy on top of your existing covers.

As you stitch, keep in mind that our imaginations easily fill any void. It's partially up to us whether we fill these spaces with beautiful fields of poppies or sharp-toothed villains. Try to imagine pleasant, calming scenes while you knit, as these make it much easier to fall asleep.

Sleepyhead

Since you will be forming sleepy stitches, I recommend using a very simple throw pattern. In fact, I even recommend not using a pattern at all. Just knit a throw-size glob of garter stitch back and forth on round needles. A gauge of 4 or 5 stitches per inch using worsted-weight yarn on size US 7 to 9 needles will decrease the likelihood of accidentally dropping stitches and will make for a thick, warm throw.

After completing each stitch, slide your thumb in between the first and second stitch on the left needle. Having your thumb there will help you guide the right-hand needle to the proper place to enter the next stitch.

It's Okay to Be in the Dark

Are you nervous about dropping stitches in the dark? It's important to keep the lights off if you want to fall back asleep, so you will simply have to work with the darkness. I've found that knitting is as much about feel as sight, and I bet that you will drop fewer stitches than you expect. Even so, give yourself permission to drop a stitch here and there without fixing it. (It's not worth turning the light on!) Let your friendly monster be a little bit strange looking, just as any monster should be. You will find that letting go of perfect knitting will only give your monster more character, charm, and authenticity.

Knitting at the Movies

Making a friendly monster might turn you into an expert at knitting in the dark. If so, you may also come to enjoy other perks, such as the option to knit in movie theaters, while camping, or as a clickety passenger in a car at night.

play-by-PLAY

M Y FEELINGS ABOUT SPORTS can be summed up by confessing the fact that my favorite part of childhood soccer games was the fresh orange slices at halftime. Similarly, the best thing about a pack of baseball cards was the stick of gum. Whether playing or watching, I've always been rather indifferent about the whole thing, especially the winning and losing. I'm much more interested in making scarves than scoring goals. I'd rather learn a new stitch pattern than sketch out a new offense strategy.

So, what is a nonenthusiast like me to do when her loved one — brother, spouse, child, niece — is out there on the field giving it his or her all? Or perhaps you're already so enthused about the hustle and action that you've just got to do more? Join in with needles and yarn, and make your own game of it. I invite you to turn yourself into a live commentator, using stitches instead of words, and to find a reason to care more than ever about each goal and point, hoot and holler.

Become a sports commentator, using stitches instead of words.

There are many different ways to commentate with needles and yarn. Some are more appropriate for certain sports than others. Here are a few examples. Feel free to mix and match, or invent your own! If you only want to commentate for one game, make something small like a baby hat or hand warmers (for pattern, see page 151). If you want to track a whole season, make a scarf or a sweater. (For scarf sizes, see page 164.)

Take Me Out to the Ball Game

Take two balls of yarn to the ballpark, one for each team's color. Knit in stockinette stitch in the appropriate color while each team is at bat. (For a scarf, work 3 or 4 stitches in garter stitch along both edges to prevent the fabric from curling.) Switch colors when the teams switch sides. Since the often-slow pace of baseball means that runs can be few and far between, choose something more frequent to commentate on. For each strike, work a few stitches to create a ridge, like a strike line on a scorecard. (Be sure to purl when you're on the knit side and knit if you're on the purl side so that you create the appropriate ridge in the field of stockinette.) Each time a team scores a run, knit a bobble — the shape of a baseball — in that team's color. All along and in between these events, keep knitting in stockinette stitch. The final garment will reveal the contours of the game, a soft and fuzzy statistical record. (For how to knit a bobble, see page 138.)

Match Point: Tennis

For tennis, choose just one color of yarn, perhaps green like the court or fluorescent yellow like the ball. Then, simply knit 1 stitch each time the ball is hit. Follow the action in real time, moving your head side to side, stitch by stitch. Pay close attention to the aesthetics of each shot. Whenever you witness a clean winner or a remarkable diving volley, for example, knit a bobble. When a player serves up an ace, knit a bobble. When a player smiles or laughs and is a good sport, knit a bobble. The final garment will show each outstanding moment against a smooth ground of still-impressive forehands and backhands.

A Slam Dunk: Basketball

In contrast to baseball and tennis, a typical basketball game contains a lot of scoring. How can our needles ever hope to keep up with the pace? I recommend knitting or purling based on which team has possession of the ball at any given moment. Before you begin, decide which team will be knit and which team will be purl. Let a pattern emerge spontaneously as you try to keep up with this fast-paced game. You might find yourself sweating along with the players on the court! Wear a 1970s-style headband as needed.

navigating by HEART

I F I CLOSE MY EYES FOR A FEW MINUTES, I can conjure up the front yard of my childhood home. And once there, I can either do cart-wheels or strap on my roller skates and go any number of places: my best friend's house, the ice cream shop on Main Street, or my elementary school. I left that little beach town in Southern California 20 years ago, but I still know those routes by heart. I also remember precisely how to get from my college dorm room to my then-boyfriend's apartment: go downstairs, exit, take a left, pass the tree we climbed together, cross the creek, work my way along the edge of campus, cross a busy street, continue straight, turn left at the community garden, and go one more short block. In my memory, he is still there waiting for me to arrive, and I am about to knock on his front door.

Knowing something — a route, a song, a phone number — by heart is a sign that something is important to us. These things sink deep into our memory, so deep that we can forget they are still there. With this project, I invite you to be your own personal archaeologist and to unearth a beloved route in your memory. We'll commemorate our old stomping grounds by knitting scarves that double as directions, marking each right or left turn using short-row wraps.

Walk down Memory Lane

Your first task is to dip back into time with your imagination. Close your eyes and recall the places you have lived. Let your mind wander until your heart snags upon a particular activity, relationship, or detail. Ask if there is a frequent route associated with those memories. If at first you can only vaguely recall what was between point A and point B, do not despair. If you keep your eyes closed and try again to retrace your steps, you'll likely remember at least a few key turns.

Imagine, then knit, a well-worn route that brings back special memories.

Once you have the essence of the route in mind, pick up a pencil and a blank piece of paper. Draw a single line that captures the major curves, sharp turns, and straightaways in between point A and point B. Then, surround the line by sketching a border around it, so it's enclosed in an irregular rectangle with the proper proportions for a scarf. Lastly, go back with a different colored pencil and highlight the spots where the route deviates from a straight path; these are the areas where you will use short rows to shape the scarf. (For how to work short rows, see page 156.) Knit your scarf in any yarn, gauge, and color you like.

Mapmaking Option

If you would prefer a scarf based on a scientifically accurate representation of your special route, simply obtain a map of your beloved place and trace the route with a thick marker so it stands out. Then surround the route so that it's enclosed in a scarf-proportioned rectangle, as on the opposite page, and continue as above.

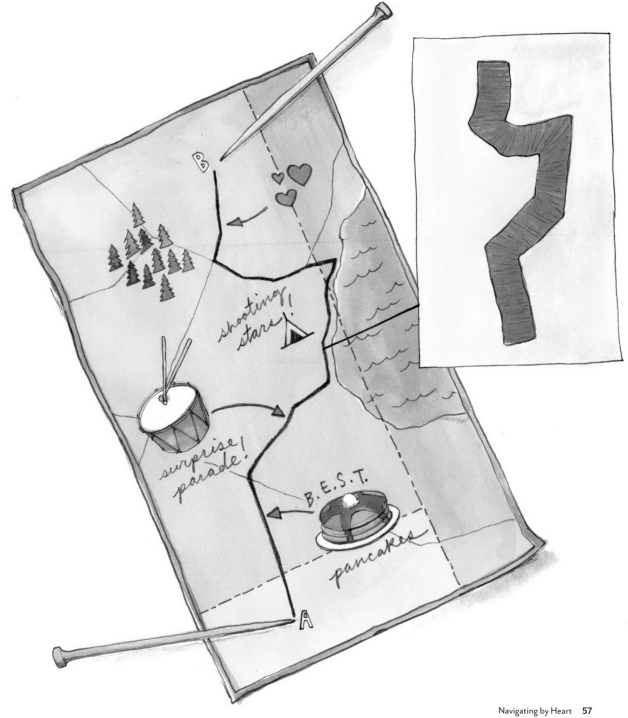

inching UP

P ART OF BEING A CHILD is accepting, even celebrating, the passage of time from a wonderfully naïve perspective. Another birthday already? One hundred percent hooray! Older. Bigger. Better. For adults, on the other hand, such celebrations are more often bittersweet. There is a direct correlation between our enthusiasm about getting older and our ability to communicate our age by holding up the number on our fingers.

Lingering in my memories of the house I grew up in is the faint image of a doorframe with hand-drawn notches working their way up the side. Next to some of the notches are my first name and the date, scrawled in whatever handwriting style I cultivated that year. The others track my older (and taller) brother's progress over the course of his childhood. Despite whatever hopes I might have entertained as a small child, it has been clear for quite some time now that I will never catch up to him. As we inched our way up the doorframe, we also grew up in other ways, until at some point we didn't even notice that we had stopped keeping track of our height.

Celebrate the growth of a special child from birth to 18 years old.

Instead of marking notches on a doorframe, you will slowly knit a scarf as you track the height of an important child in your life (child, grand-child, niece or nephew, friend's child). When the child turns 18, you will gift the scarf to the person in celebration of his or her transition to adulthood. Make this a special occasion, perhaps the day she goes off to college, or the day he moves out of his parents' home and gets his first apartment.

The Inch-by-Inch Scarf

This scarf can be made in place of, or in addition to, a chart on a real doorframe. Just think how much easier it is to transport a yarn chart than one scrawled on a doorframe if the family moves to a new home! Here are three different variations, ranging from aesthetically subtle to bold, for you to consider before you decide exactly how to proceed with your own version. When choosing yarn, keep in mind that while you begin by knitting for a baby, you will end by knitting for an adult; I recommend resisting any temptations to begin with baby colors if you want your future 18-year-old to be willing to wear the scarf. (For standard scarf widths and stitch counts, see pages 163–164.)

- **VERSION 1.** Knit in a different color for each year. Choose the first color and knit the scarf until it is the length of the child at birth. Use any stitch pattern you like. On the child's first birthday, choose a second color and add inches to the scarf until it matches the child's height on that day. Continue adding a block of new color to the scarf each year after measuring the child's growth progress on each birthday until age 18.

- **VERSION 2.** Make a two-color scarf. Begin by knitting the child's birth length with color #1, using any stitch pattern of your choice, then knit a thin stripe of color #2 to represent the day the child was born. When the child turns 1 year old, add inches in color #1 to match the first birthday height, followed by another thin stripe of color #2 to mark the birthday. In this version, the final scarf is mostly color #1, with 19 thin stripes showing the height at each birthday from birth to age 18. Bind off on his or her 18th birthday, just after the last stripe.

- **VERSION 3.** Make a one-color scarf with more subtle height marks. This works like the previous version, except instead of making each birthday with a second color, mark them with a contrasting stitch pattern, such as a thin ridge in garter stitch on a field of stockinette.

Notch It Up
Consider adding another little "notch" at each inch mark along the scarf, turning the whole thing into a true measuring tool and making it possible to know the actual height at each birthday by counting the notches. The notch could be incorporated along one edge of the scarf with a contrasting color or stitch pattern.

The Finishing Touch
When you gift-wrap the finished scarf, tie a big bow around the parcel with a fabric measuring tape instead of a typical ribbon.

HEIRLOOM *time traveler*

M Y TRUSTY KNITTING-NEEDLE CASE was once my grandmother's, and before it was hers, it belonged to my great-grandmother. I don't know if she bought it new or if there's yet another story lost to time. I do know that my grandmother often used to tell me that her mother would have been very proud of my knitting, especially my even tension. I only faintly remember my great-grandmother, who passed away when I was just a wee one. Oh, how I wish we three could have knit side by side!

I imagine that most heirlooms are accidents. As far as I know, my great-grandmother did not specifically intend for me to have her needle case, though I trust she would be delighted that I do. My grandmother's berry baskets, which now hang in my kitchen as heirlooms in the making, were certainly not originally purchased for that purpose. And yet, might it be a lovely thing to intentionally begin an heirloom, to set out from the beginning with one's descendants in mind? How might I knit with a yet-to-be great-grandchild whose lifetime might not overlap with mine at all?

Imagine that you stumble upon a cedar box in your grandparents' attic. You blow the dust off the top, revealing a label that reads "Open this box in 2014. Sealed with love in 1914." The box has warped a bit, but you manage to pry the lid off. Inside you find a sealed envelope and a scarf still on needles, unfinished. You open the letter. It is from your great-grandmother, and she wrote it to a yet-to-be-born you. She

explains that the half-finished scarf is intended for you to complete and that she will keep you company as you stitch. She acknowledges that you might not even know how to knit, but she hopes you might learn or that you will pass the project on to another family member to enjoy. Her initials are knit into the beginning of the scarf, and she invites whoever completes it to knit his or her own initials into the other end.

This project is surely a grand act of optimism. If you begin this heirloom scarf, you will never know how the story unfolds. I believe it is worth a try, just in case it goes well.

Knit Something Beautiful

You may knit your half of the scarf with any yarn, gauge, and color of your choosing. Most importantly, knit something that is beautiful to you. It should communicate something — however subtle — about who you are. When you box up the half-knit scarf, be sure to include enough extra yarn for it to be finished 100 years later. (The yarn shop will certainly be out of that dye lot by then!)

There are many ways to incorporate lettering into knitting. Since this is a scarf and both sides will show, I recommend doing the letters in such a way that they look good on both sides, simply using contrasting pattern stitches. For example, if you are knitting in garter stitch, you could do the letters in stockinette. Or vice versa. I like to do letters by first sketching them out on graph paper. For standard scarf sizes and information about stitch counts and yarn weights, see pages 163–164.

Perfect Planning

Ensuring the material preservation of this project is absolutely essential. One hundred years in a paper or plastic bag will not treat your handwork well. A cedar box makes an ideal time capsule for yarn because it repels moths. Be sure to also get a tight seal so insects cannot crawl in and munch on your scarf.

A Letter from the Past

Wouldn't it be amazing to read a hand-written letter from a great-grandparent? When you are writing the letter that will accompany the scarf in progress, feel free to be elaborate and verbose. Choose special stationery and write with your favorite pen. Your descendant is likely to cherish every word.

For More than One

If you want to cover your bases, just in case you have multiple great-grandchildren who like to knit, you can seal up multiple half-knit scarves inside the cedar time capsule.

you are as beautiful as the MOON

YA AMAR IS A WAY TO SAY "You are beautiful" to someone in Arabic. This compliment, literally and quite poetically, translates to "like the moon." What might it mean to knit like the moon and to wear a garment that somehow glows? When I don't know where to begin, I often conduct research. It seems to go best when I have no particular goal in mind. I just gather facts and stories and keep a list of all the tidbits that pull at my heartstrings along the way. I don't worry about where it is taking me. I just trust the process and follow my intuition.

Dinosaurs and Moon Cakes

A recent round of research of all things related to the moon uncovered the above *ya amar* saying in addition to the following snippets:

- Tycho, the brightest crater on the moon, is named after the Danish astronomer Tycho Brahe (1546–1601). It is 85 kilometers wide and an estimated 108 million years old. Dinosaurs could have observed the moment of impact that created it.

- The most detailed lunar map of the 19th century was hand-drawn by the German astronomer Johann Friedrich Julius Schmidt. With 32,856 craters, it contains an extraordinary amount of detail and reflects remarkable patience.

- Moon gardens are filled with night-blooming plants and nocturnal insects. The blooms of plants such as the twining moonflower and the toxic angel's trumpet only stay open until touched by sunlight.

- Before science proved otherwise, there was an era of literary fantasy about life on the moon. In 1657, the French satirist Cyrano de Bergerac imagined that, on the moon, birds talked and people used poetry as currency instead of coins.

- The moon's orbit is not perfectly circular, and the moon is not perfectly spherical.

- Footprints made by Neil Armstrong and Buzz Aldrin on the moon in 1969 are still there. Since the moon has no wind or rain, and very little geological surface activity, they are likely to be perfectly preserved there for a very, very long time.

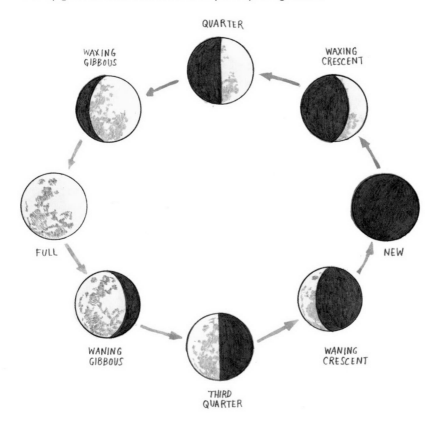

- At the Chinese Moon Festival, people eat moon cakes (with lotus-seed filling) and gaze at the moon. If they are geographically separated from their relatives, they can at least enjoy the fact that they are watching the same moon that night.

In the Round

What might these moon-related findings mean for knitting? What can I knit that is in the spirit of these facts? And not just *what* can I knit, but also *how* shall I knit it? And not just how shall I *knit* it, but how might I enjoy *wearing* it? How can every "small step" of the way be infused with moonlight?

My first instinct is to knit something round, like the shape of the moon, its orbit, and its cyclical phases. It should be knit in the round as well, on circular needles, so that the movement of my stitching is orbit-like. These thoughts lead me to the idea of a cowl. (For a circular-knit cowl pattern, see pages 155–156.) In honor of Johann Friedrich Julius Schmidt, let's imagine that each stitch, each tiny loop, is a crater.

Knit a double-sided cowl, with a white side representing the portion of the moon that is illuminated and the other side black for the part in shadow. For example, when the moon is a thin crescent, turn it so that it shows mostly black and just a little bit of white.

THIRD QUARTER

WAXING CRESCENT

WANING GIBBOUS

Wax and Wane

Keep an eye on the current phase of the moon, and as you wear the finished cowl, rotate it so that the ratio of white to black corresponds to the ratio of illumination to shadow on the current moon that evening.

A waning gibbous would be mostly white and a little bit of black. *Ya amar!*

hummingbird HEARTBEAT

I HAVE AN ASSIGNMENT FOR YOU. Close your eyes and place your hand on your wrist or chest to find your heartbeat. As you do, think about the fact that there are more than seven billion other human hearts beating right now alongside yours. Listen closely to your own heartbeat for a few moments while you imagine the other seven billion joining in — only a few at first, then many, many more. Perhaps visualize a globe and trace your attention around it, letting never-to-be-met individuals in the midst of their diverse daily routines pop into view. While this activity might bring to mind how very small each of us is, for me, the stronger feeling is one of profound connection. It is the ever-present chorus of our common humanity.

Hummingbird ~ 1,250

Cat ~ 150

Dog ~ 90

I have another assignment for you. Since humans are not the only significant creatures on this planet, return to your own heartbeat, but this time imagine trillions of other animal heartbeats joining the pulse of humanity. These beats vary in tempo. Generally, the smaller the animal, the more heartbeats per minute pulsing through its body. While a human's heart at rest typically beats 60 to 80 times per minute, a hummingbird's can beat up to 1,250 times per minute. On the other end of the spectrum, a blue whale's heart beats just 6 times per minute. An elephant's rate is 30, and that of a lively little squirrel is, unsurprisingly, about 280. What might all these numbers mean for knitting?

Monkey – 192

Elephant – 30

Horse – 44

Blue Whale – 6

Giraffe – 65

Rabbit – 205

Squirrel – 280

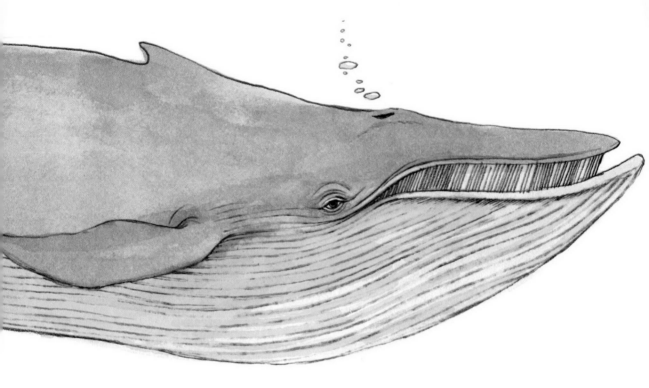

Beats per Minute

One of the things I have always enjoyed about knitting is the math of it, both the practice and the poetry of the numbers. Cold, hard facts and stats are rarely just that; if we look closely, we can almost always find the heart of things. I invite you to marvel at all these numbers with me by choosing an animal that you hold dear and knitting the animal's heart rate into the design.

I have a special fondness for hummingbirds, so, using laceweight ruby-red yarn (in honor of the ruby-throated hummingbird), I translated their 1,250 beats per minute visually into a scarf as delicate and lightweight as a hummingbird herself. I decided to knit on size US 0 needles so that my scarf would have tens of thousands of tiny stitches representing a total of about one half hour of hummingbird heartbeats. Each ruby-red stitch represents one heartbeat, and between each set of 1,250 stitches (25 rows of 50 stitches each) — or one minute's worth of hummingbird heartbeats — I knit one thin stripe in teal.

I wrapped a ruby-red scarf around my neck, composed of one half-hour's worth of hummingbird heartbeats, one stitch per beat.

I chose a scarf as the perfect garment for this idea so that I could become ruby-throated myself when I wore it. What would be the best knitted form to complement the animal you choose for your own heartbeat-inspired project? (For information about stitch counts and yarn weights, see pages 163–164.)

SUN *salutation*

I SET MY ALARM CLOCK for 5:30 A.M. and place my yarn and needles on the bedside table. I am a night owl, and getting up at that hour is not easy. In the morning, I know I will turn over to press the snooze button, but hopefully the sight of my yarn will remind me of my plan, and I will get up instead of sinking back under my covers. If all goes well, I will cast on before the crack of dawn and be ready and waiting by my east-facing window. Or better yet, I will be sitting on my roof. I will keep my eyes on the horizon, and at the precise moment when the sun peeks over the hills, I salute it with my stitches.

A circle shape, knit using the intarsia technique (see pages 160–161), will quickly grow on the wooden horizon of my needles, mimicking the sunrise in real time. As the day begins to take shape, I will greet the center of our solar system with all the attention I can muster. Whether the sun is capable of receiving thanks or not doesn't really matter; the point is to give it all the same. I will bow, needles in hand, as the sun's light soaks into the plants, making my current favorite color — green — possible. As I do, this phenomenal star that sustains life on Earth will also make its way into my knitting.

Beginning at dawn, I will greet the day by beginning a scarf that mirrors the arc of the sun in real time.

After the intarsia circle is complete and the real sun has risen, I will continue to chase the path of the sun in stitches for the rest of the day, adding row after row, trying to keep up with the growing space between

the real sun and the horizon where it rose. At midday, when the sun is overhead, my scarf should be about halfway done. I'll persevere just like the real sun, finishing the whole thing just as the sun sinks into the Pacific. One day. One scarf. In the final few inches, I will incorporate a slit, like a giant buttonhole, as the "sunset." As I wrap the scarf around my neck at nightfall, I will "set" my handknit sun by sinking it into the slit. (For instructions on how to knit the slit, see pages 144–145.) One more tip: don't forget your sunblock!

Stitches per Day

I recommend making a test swatch ahead of time to be sure that the weight and gauge of the yarn you choose allow you to knit the whole scarf in just one day. To do this, use scrap yarn and cast on the correct number of stitches you need for the scarf width you're aiming for. (For advice about standard scarf sizes, stitch counts, and yarn weights, see pages 163–164.) Knit on your swatch for one half hour straight, then multiply the length of that swatch by two and then by the number of hours you expect to make available the day you plan to "salute" the sun. If the result isn't long enough for your satisfaction, either choose a heavier yarn (and larger needles) or simply increase the size of your needles (for a lacier effect with the same yarn), either way resulting in fewer rows per inch. For example, my swatch tests helped me decide to knit my scarf with size US 11 needles. The resulting gauge let me knit about 4 inches per hour as I chased the sun across the sky.

Shades of Sunshine

You can knit a yellow sun into a solid sky-blue scarf if you like, or feel free to mix things up. I recommend knitting the circle as a warm color (for example, yellow, orange, or pink) and the rest of the scarf in a contrasting cool color (such as blue, green, or purple), just so the sun stands out nicely. If you want to get a little fancier, you could even vary the sky colors over the course of the day, such as creating a radiant sunrise of pinks, oranges, even purples. Of course, obtaining these sunrise skeins ahead of time doesn't guarantee you a vibrant sunrise; I recommend collecting an array of possible sunrise colors, keeping your receipt, and not removing the skein labels until you know you'll use them on the day of your sun salutation. Then, on the big day, let the sky dictate your scarf's overture.

Vista Points

- If your home doesn't provide a good view of the sunrise, go someplace special for the day where you'll have a better view. Perhaps seek out a coastal view, hike to a mountaintop, or take an elevator to the top of a tall building. The most important thing is that you can actually see the sun as it rises and sets. This might mean observing the sunrise from one location and then traveling to another spot at some point during the day to catch a good view of the sunset.

- If you want a longer scarf, or more hours to make it, do this project as close as possible to the summer solstice to maximize the number of hours of daylight.

Rise and Shine

Instead of spending a whole day knitting a scarf, knit a sunny bedspread on a series of mornings, each day working a sun into a square of whatever size you'd like. Piece these sunrises together into a bedspread along the way. When it is complete, your bedspread full of suns will greet you every morning, reminding you to honor the day. This patchwork bedspread would look fabulous if knit with a series of diverse color combos; there is no need to stick to a yellow sun and blue sky with every square!

BUTTERFLY *birthday*

IMAGINE THAT IT IS YOUR BIRTHDAY. All week, small parcels have been appearing in your mailbox. The packages all have the words *Time Flies* written on the outside, even though they are from different senders. The official day is finally here, so you open the little bundles at breakfast. Each package releases a flurry of handknit butterflies into your kitchen, just for you on your birthday!

As a special gift, create a lovely set of butterfly-adorned placemats, one knit by each person in a group of friends and relatives.

Upon closer inspection, and a careful reading of the cards and notes that accompany the parcels, you learn that the number of little 1-inch butterflies on each placemat has significance. Each friend who made you a placemat has incorporated one little butterfly into it for each year that she has known you. The one from your oldest friend might have 26 butterflies, while the one from your sister-in-law has 8. Each is unique, just like each relationship.

The set reminds you that a birthday always means another opportunity to grow and change in beautiful ways. A human life can transform many times, and while we may not have a new pair of colorful wings to show for it each time, human transformation is both as common and as extraordinary as the metamorphosis of a caterpillar. As we creatively adapt to our ever-changing situations, our loved ones encourage us to get out of our chrysalides and spread our wings.

If you imagine that it would be wonderful to receive this set of butterfly placemats, the good news is that it is also a joy to give it. When you and your friends drop your packages off at the post office, you can delight

in the poetic liveliness of the collective gift you are sending. All week, you can look up into the sky and imagine the butterflies on the placemat you knit, excitedly flapping their wings in the direction of your friend's house. Even if you might see your friend in person on her birthday, you should still send this gift via postal mail. The fresh air is good for the butterflies.

Organize the Surprise

The first necessity is a project coordinator. Perhaps you? This person will need to secretly spread the word to the birthday girl's friends and family members who knit. For consistency and to keep the focus on the different number of butterflies on each placemat, it's best to knit them all in the same color — coordinated with the birthday girl's taste and dining room, if possible. To make sure everyone purchases the proper yarn, either buy it all at once and send a skein to each knitter, or let them know the brand, color, and weight. Select an easy-to-find brand so they can purchase it in their local yarn shop.

Linen is a classic fiber choice for a tabletop textile, so I recommend working with sport- or worsted-weight linen yarn, although a cotton-linen blend is also very nice. Linen ages well, just like friendships, and it will get softer and softer over the years.

Give the knitters plenty of lead time, including a recommended shipping deadline, and be sure they all know the date of the birthday. You might want to give a few encouraging reminders along the way. Also, to ensure that all the placemats are opened on the same day, have everyone write *Time Flies* and *Open on Your Birthday!* on the outside of the shipping parcels.

You'll find knitting instructions for both sport- and worsted-weight linen (or linen-blend) placemats on pages 159–160. Make sure everyone has the pattern, and be ready to give technical advice if necessary.

Planning Ahead

If you want to plan the layout of the butterflies before you begin, I recommend simply cutting a piece of paper to the exact dimensions of the placemat, with lines indicating the Seed Stitch border around all four sides. Put an X where you'd like each butterfly to be within that frame. Then, as you knit, you can simply hold your in-process placemat up to the paper template at any time to see if it's time to begin another butterfly.

Right on Time

Start organizing early for this project, and allow plenty of time for shipping. It's okay if the parcels pile up at the birthday girl's house a week before the big day. Better early than late!

string of PEARLS

I AM ALWAYS ON THE LOOKOUT for the poetry hiding inside things. I try to be ready for the moments when the mundane slips into the extraordinary and things can be seen or experienced anew. I am thinking of the lovely moment when I realized that a pinch of salt feels like Braille dots between my fingertips. Since then, I have enjoyed sprinkling tiny poetic crystals on my breakfast eggs. For me, an insight like this is a rare gem. I polish up these moments and hold on tight. They are the deep-sea pearls that I collect and string together.

I imagine that diving for real pearls feels much the same. For centuries, pearl hunters have held their breath and plunged deep into shark-infested waters in search of these jewels of the sea. Their value comes from their rarity. Only one in 10,000 wild oysters holds an exquisite iridescent orb. And each pearl can take up to 20 years to form, depending on its size and whether it is a freshwater or saltwater specimen.

Authentic pearls are wild accidents; oysters make them as a protective response to tiny intruders between their shells. Being in the right place at the right time, these specks get covered with layer upon layer of nacre, the rainbow-like material that lines the insides of oyster shells.

Authentic poetry is also a wild accident, or at least it feels that way. No matter how much I might try, and no matter how many moments I drag up to the surface and pry open, to hold a pearly idea in the palm of my hand is always a gift. Really all I can do is this: approach every person, place, and thing with the assumption that there *might* be a pearl hiding inside, but that I cannot know ahead of time. So I pay close attention and try to be ready.

Since I am a knitter, thinking about pearls inevitably leads to one word: bobble.

So, that's it. Simple. I will knit bobbles based on personal experience all the while knitting a delightful linen hand towel. Each time I stumble upon a poetic moment in my everyday life, I will form a little linen "pearl" in a sea of stockinette. A one-color towel should be easy to carry around with me, so I can add each bobble while the moment is fresh. Since pearls are rare, I will need to be discerning when deciding which moments make the cut. Most of the time, I will knit in plain old humdrum stockinette, letting the bobbles stand out. A relatively fine gauge is required so that there is plenty of time for a rare bobble to punctuate the plain background. (A fine gauge will also make a lovely towel to hang in a home.) I can play with the size of the bobbles; they can be made with as few as 3 stitches and as many as 9. Each additional stitch of a bobble is like another layer of nacre, forming a bigger, more valuable "pearl." To keep the edges of the stockinette-stitch towel from rolling over, work a border of Seed Stitch all around: knit 5 rows of Seed Stitch before beginning the stockinette, as well as before you bind off, and knit 5 stitches in Seed Stitch along each edge. (For instructions on how to knit bobbles, see page 138; for stockinette and Seed Stitch, see pages 136–137.)

Rare Gems

What is your version of the few and far between? What extraordinariness might you like to track more closely as you make a lovely linen hand towel? It is likely that the moments you care to gather are different from mine, and it is important that you choose something that is uniquely you. Perhaps it will be kind acts observed. Or maybe it will be letters received in the mail. A whole day with one's cell phone turned off would certainly qualify. What are the rare things that you cherish?

Everyday Reminder

Whether you make one linen hand towel or a whole heap of them, let these bobbles hang in your home as a reminder of the way a seemingly lackluster moment can suddenly produce an exquisite pearl. Let the texture of the towel in your hands remind you to keep your eyes open to the ever-possible extraordinariness that hides deep within.

QUANTUM
entanglement

KNITTING CAN BE A GREAT THING TO DO while waiting for a bus, a friend, or a dentist appointment. It's easy to sneak in a few rows here and there, and, all of a sudden, you've finished another project! But there are other kinds of waiting — of the heart-wrenching, stomach-churning kind. And it is one of these instances that led to this next project. In this case, I happened to be waiting on a man. I was ready; he was hesitant. He had a good point: we lived 3,095 miles apart. But I had a good point, too: we were obviously quite fond of each other. And this particular gentleman happened to love neckties. And knots. My theory is that knotting a tie around his collar lets him feel like a sailor, a scout, and a dapper man all at once. He wears them even when he doesn't have to. It was decided: a necktie in his favorite color, safety orange.

This idea grew out of my need for a concrete project into which I could channel my emotions while I waited to see what would unfold.

This man and I have conversations about quantum mechanics that mostly go over my head, but one night the concept of quantum entanglement came up and made a surprising amount of sense to me. I decided to knit him a tie inspired by the lovely idea that tiny bits of matter infinitely far apart are actually connected in mysterious, seemingly impossible ways. I knit a cable down the tie, incorporating traveling stitches so that the two cable lines split apart and met in the middle, again and again, as if they were dancing across the universe. I had trouble figuring out the cable on my own, so I did some online research, at which point I discovered that this particular cable happens to be called an Hourglass Cable. How unbelievably perfect! I would knit hourglasses as I waited.

On the day I started the tie, I knew that I might never finish it or give it to him. But that was beside the point; starting it was what mattered. I was knitting for me as much as for him. My anxious heart needed an activity to stay calm, a place to put the love that he was not ready to receive. I have taken breaks from working on the tie, but I seem to keep coming back to it, adding a few more rows while thinking of him. Someday, will it be his favorite tie? And perhaps someday . . .

The Waiting Game

If you're waiting for something or someone, however calmly or anxiously, consider knitting Hourglass Cables into whatever you are making. A scarf? The arms of a sweater? A necktie for a love interest? You'll find many versions of this classic cable, but the one I used is on pages 157–158. If you make a tie, it's best to use as fine a yarn as you are comfortable working with, perhaps lace-weight with US 0 needles.

K1, B1
(knit one, breathe one)

A *mudra* is a spiritual gesture performed with the hands. Hundreds of different hand positions, each with a unique symbolism, are found on ancient statues of the Buddha. Today, mudras are still part of ceremonies, dances, and meditation practices in a variety of religions, including Hinduism and Buddhism. For example, the *dhyana mudra*, often used in Buddhist meditation, typically is formed by relaxing the hands in one's lap, the right hand on top of the left with both palms facing upward, and letting the tips of the thumbs gently touch each other.

Meditation is not something at which I am particularly adept. As soon as I ask all the things in my head to chill out and take a break, they loop back around stronger than ever. They seem to love teasing me. I suppose this is all the more reason to meditate, or at least to try. I would certainly like to hone my ability to choose my thoughts, rather than letting them choose me. While I admire the approach of sitting quietly and simply focusing on one's breath, honestly, it just doesn't seem to work for me. I need something outside of me to arrest my attention. Can yarn and needles help?

Might a mudra of sorts have been hiding in my knitting practice all along?

If so, I have been an accidental meditator for decades, and perhaps a slightly more skilled one than I thought. I do not doubt that the calming aspect of knitting comes at least partially from the way it draws my attention to what is right in front of me. If the needle on the left is the past and the needle on the right is the future, the particular stitch between my two needles is always precisely the present moment.

Here is a knitting-based meditation practice that I have designed and begun to experiment with. Perhaps you would like to give it a try? At the end, there is an unexpected, yet entirely appropriate, twist. You might resist it (I certainly do), but that is perfectly understandable and partly the point.

Provisions

To begin, choose an appropriate yarn. I recommend a color that is calming, perhaps a light blue. A smooth texture that feels pleasant as it slips through your fingers is also a good idea. It helps to knit in a gauge that is large enough to be relatively easy. I like using a worsted-weight merino yarn on size US 9 needles.

Garter stitch is the ideal choice for this project, saving you from having to remember to switch knits and purls for a more complicated pattern. You can cast on however many stitches you like; I recommend 20. (See page 136 for garter stitch.)

Begin Your Practice

Find a comfortable place to sit that has as few distractions as possible. Perhaps you would like to sit cross-legged. Set a timer for 30 minutes. When you are settled, begin to cast on, and as you do, pay close attention to the movement of your hands. Try to conjure up a sense of your hands performing a spiritual — or at least beautiful — gesture. Notice the feel of the yarn as it slides through your fingers. Notice your breath. Here's where the K1, B1 comes in. As you enter your needle into the first stitch, also breathe in through your nose; breathe out through your mouth as you finish that same stitch, lifting it off the needle. This will likely lead you to knit more slowly than usual. Let the speed of your stitching be determined by whatever breathing speed is comfortable for you.

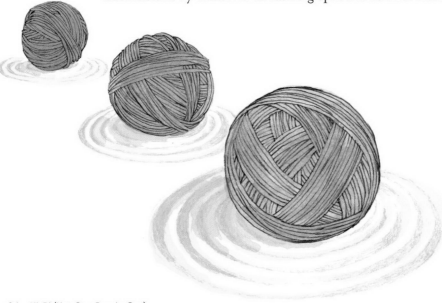

When thoughts pull your attention away from your handwork, try to notice the thoughts, gently set them aside, and refocus on your hands. At times you are likely to get distracted and lose sync. If it happens often, perhaps purl 1 stitch to help you consciously redirect. All along, be gentle with yourself. The number of times you purl is something to notice, but not to judge.

When your timer rings, your session is almost over. The final step: unravel it. Yes, unravel the entire thing. Wind the yarn back into a ball, ready and waiting for your next session.

Make Timers

Prepare the yarn in a special way, making "timers" in the form of yarn balls of various sizes. These will serve as a material reminder of your practice. Make a 10-minute ball, a 30-minute ball, and, if you're feeling ambitious, a 1-hour ball as well — a true hourglass. To determine how big these balls of yarn should be, simply cut the yarn at the end of your first meditation session of each of these durations. You will end up with yarns of three different lengths; I find that my 10-minute ball is about the size of a robin's egg. These balls will keep time for you naturally during future sessions. Having different increments gives you options for sessions of varying lengths.

grandmother's basket of BERRIES

M Y CHILDHOOD SUMMERS usually included a trip to my grandparents' house in the Appalachians of North Carolina. Alongside knitting lessons, shucking wormy ears of corn, and epic games of Rummi-Q, there was always wild-berry picking. I'm undecided on which was the bigger treat: eventually eating the berries or choosing an empty basket from my grandmother's special collection hanging in the dining room before heading out. Each basket — small, unique, and precious — was crafted with care out of natural fibers. Making them required an attention to detail similar to that required to be a good berry picker. Baskets in hand, we would slowly walk the mountain roads plucking nature's handiwork, one sweet juicy bobble at a time.

I have a photo of my grandmother Mary Ann teaching eight-year-old me to knit: two straight needles held by four warm hands. In it, I am wearing a sweater she made for me. Whoever spontaneously snapped that Polaroid could not have predicted what it would mean to me when I stumbled upon it 20 years later. I remember exactly what it was like to knit with my grandmother in the middle of a thunderstorm with a tummy full of wildberry cobbler. I didn't even have to worry if I dropped a stitch; she had me covered. And she still has me covered today, as I patiently pick up my own dropped stitches just like she taught me, her smile now on my face.

This berry-picking-inspired knitting project helps family feel close even when they are geographically scattered.

Grandmother gets a golden-colored hat in Basketweave Stitch (page 139), and each grandchild gets a red hat knit in Raspberry Stitch (page 139). When all the little berry hats are finished and tucked inside grandmother's larger "basket" hat, it is as if she is holding and hugging all the grandchildren at once. You might want to gift them all to grandmother first and let her pass out the rest. Be sure to put name tags on them so the right child gets the right size!

Onto Your Needles

Since these hats are covered in patterned stitches (Basketweave and Raspberry Stitch), it's important to knit them in a way that preserves the patterning. I suggest knitting a straight tube hat with no shaping at the top. (You'll find a pattern on pages 149–150.) Once the knitting is completed, you close the opening by simply gathering the stitches together and fastening off inside.

My, How You've Grown!

If you're going to knit many hats for your set, keep in mind that children grow quickly! Consider knitting the first hats a bit big so that those children haven't outgrown their hats before you finish the set and give them to everyone.

mind the GAP

SOMETIMES AN IDEA FOR A PROJECT hides right under my nose. How is it possible that I rode the subway for a decade before I noticed how much the rail lines on the subway map look like pieces of yarn — colors, kinks, and all? The answer has something to do with the way the mind makes meaning, especially when it is busy being sensible. I was so locked into the map as a representation of my city's subway system, something to help me get from point A to point B, that I was blinded to the simple truth that the overall image looks just like a handful of yarn scraps. Then the similarity dawned on me, as though from some sort of magical gap in the universe, and now that's all I see on subway maps all over the world — strands of colored yarn winding over rivers and across cities.

Aha! Knit with yarns that color-coordinate with the subway lines you're riding on.

Once I finally saw the subway lines as lengths of yarn, my imagination could start playing with them. In a way, this project asks you to pluck the subway lines right off the map and knit them up! Ready to ride? Do you have your ticket? We'll be knitting with yarns that match the colors of the train lines on the map, switching colors whenever we switch lines. For example, when you're on the red line, you'll knit in red; when you transfer to the blue line, you'll switch yarns and add rows in blue. As your rides accumulate on your needles over time, you will gain a bird's-eye view of the patterning of your own personal geography.

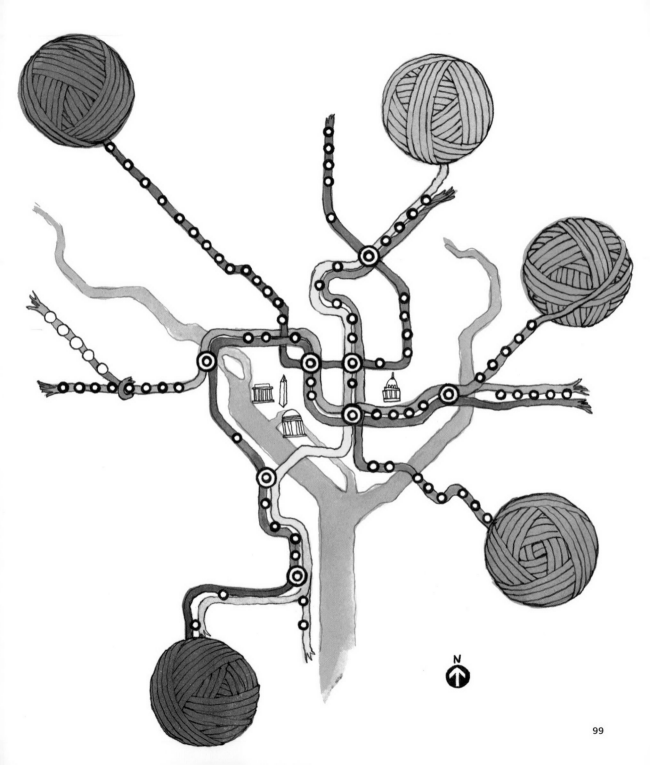

Rules of the Rail

- Only knit when the train is moving, so that the amount of fabric always corresponds to the distance traveled on a particular line. Pause whenever the train stops to let people in and out. Pause if the train breaks down. Every stitch should be a stitch in motion.

- Sometimes you might need to quickly transfer trains midrow. It's okay! Don't miss your connection. Just finish that row after you're settled on the next train and begin the next color as soon as you get back to the side where you can join the new color.

- Make a garment that reflects how much time you spend on the subway. If you rarely ride the subway, you might want to make something small like a hat so it doesn't take forever to finish it. If you ride the subway frequently, it might be interesting to make a scarf in order to collect a larger data set, possibly capturing a rare jaunt in a new neighborhood.

- If you find yourself knitting in the same one or two colors most of the time, consider planning an excursion to another part of town as a way to add diversity to your garment and, at the same time, add intrigue to your daily routine.

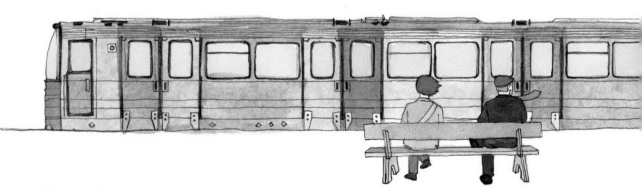

Add Map Pins

Public transportation generally packs a lot of strangers into a tight space. Things can get interesting as a result. Consider documenting observations while you are on the train. For example, you could add a bobble (page 138) every time you converse with a stranger or run into someone you know. Or, if you're knitting stockinette, work in a few purl stitches on the right side (or knit stitches on the wrong side) every time you witness someone give up his or her seat for another person who needs it. It's up to you to decide what you want to watch for and how to mark it. What part of a subway ride fascinates you?

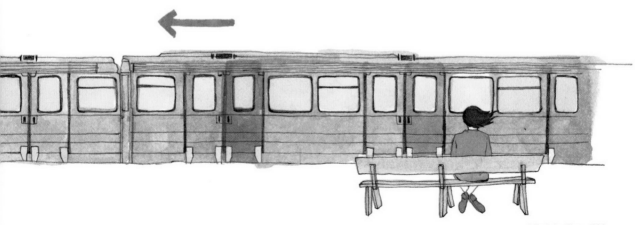

BRAVE stitches

A TRIP TO THE YARN STORE usually means a chance to discover an exciting new yarn or combination of colors. We might have some questions: Do these look good together? Will this be beautiful? But if it is 1941 and you are my grandmother, you don't want to knit in anything but brown — dull, drab brown — because it is the color of your sweetheart's uniform. In this case, there are different questions: Will this camouflage my soldier? Is it army approved? During World War II, my grandmother set aside her knack for colors and knit in solid brown so that my grandfather could blend in on the battlefield. As she knit, she anxiously waited for her love to come home. To her infinite joy, he did. Their bravery — gun in his hands and knitting needles in hers — is beyond my capacity for words. But whenever we are at a loss for words, at least there is knitting.

My grandmother's hopeful stitches, in the shapes of socks, gloves, and beanies, were much more than sweet reminders of home. They were life-or-death garments, serving an extremely practical purpose. Socks were an especially precious possession. Having enough good, dry pairs was the key to avoiding frostbite and trench foot. Soldiers would carry extra pairs inside their shirts, hoping their body heat would dry them out. Then they could swap in the fresh pair before the current ones became soaked through and dangerous. My grandmother's knitting lifted my grandfather's spirits day after day as his company fought its way across France and Belgium. I believe the two of them earned his Bronze Star together, hand in hand.

This knitting project — a pair of "decorated" socks — is in honor of my grandparents' endless courage and commitment during World War II.

This pair of socks is drab brown, of course, but with a twist. The ankles are arrayed with a colorful stripe pattern adapted from the various service ribbons earned by my grandfather during the war. While the ones I make represent a perfect fit for my grandfather's experience and recognition and his particular combination of ribbons and stripes, the project can easily be adapted to honor other servicemen and service-women — past, present, and future.

My grandfather's European–African–Middle Eastern campaign ribbon contains colored bands representing Germany, Italy, and the United States. It also contains brown and green bands, which represent the terrain of battle, ranging from beaches to woodlands. These colors, in addition to the reds, whites, and blues on the ribbon from which his Bronze Star is suspended, are featured on the ankles of the socks I am knitting.

A Private Thank-You

Given that ribbons come in long strips, my first thought for this project was to turn the service ribbon designs into long scarves. It seemed like a natural fit, except for one very important thing: my grandfather's humility. A scarf broadcasting honors earned is not my grandfather's style; he rarely talks about the war, much less his awards. It also does not resonate as well with my wish to give him a more personal, private thank-you. And then I remembered my grandmother and her sock knitting. Socks would let me honor both of their wartime deeds in a way that he could modestly cover with his pants and shoes. They would be quiet and humble, just like him. I will give this special pair of socks to my grandfather on May 8, the anniversary of Victory in Europe Day. I think he'll like them so much he may even wear them in the Arizona heat.

Planning the Design

I used a simple sock pattern (see pages 147–149) and knit the sock feet in the original army-brown that my grandfather remembers. I began the colorful stripes at the ankles. To translate your soldier's service ribbons into a series of stripes, I recommend getting out your colored pencils and sketching the sequence of stripes before you begin. You'll have a few decisions to make: In what order will you arrange the various ribbons on the ankle? Will you incorporate all of the ribbons or select an especially meaningful few? And, if you decide to incorporate many ribbons, might you need to knit in a very small gauge to allow enough rows on the ankles for all those color switches?

WALK
around the block

ONE DAY, THE POSTMAN accidentally delivered one of my neighbor's letters into my mailbox. The address on the envelope matched mine, letter for letter and number for number, save for the very last digit. The proper home for that letter was only a few doors away, but I didn't recognize the name (Nancy) in the little plastic window. I'm embarrassed to say that I probably wouldn't have recognized Nancy in person either, even if we passed each other on our mutual sidewalk. At the time, I had lived in my new neighborhood for almost a year, and this thought made me decide that it was high time to finally meet my neighbors. Since I can be a bit of an introvert, I needed a grand plan that would be so exciting that I'd forget I was being bold, the way a teenager feels when out on a late-night scavenger hunt with a pack of friends.

The plan is to slowly work my way around the block, one house, apartment, or business at a time, meeting my neighbors and knitting a cowl along the way. This cowl will take on the look and feel of my block, a little like an architectural model, but much cozier.

I'll begin with my next-door neighbors in the pretty yellow house. I'll knock on their door, and if all goes well, they'll sit with me on their porch and we'll chat while I knit an inch or so in yellow, the color of their house. When I progress to the next house and introduce myself to the woman whose mail I received by accident, I'll need to be prepared with yarn that matches the color of her house. Since I want the order of colors on the final cowl to match the order of house colors around my block, I'll need to meet my neighbors in the proper order and not skip ahead. Whenever I arrive at a corner, I'll knit a few gray rows (the color of my sidewalk) to mark the turn.

Whether it takes weeks, months, or years to knit all the way around my block, when I finally come back around to my own house, I'll add a section in the color of my house (peach). Then I'll bind off and connect my house to the very first yellow house I knit, turning the whole piece into one continuous loop, just like my block. When the cowl is finished and I wear it around my neighborhood, folks will have a great excuse to stop me and say hello. They are likely to want to try to find their hand-knit house on my cowl!

Knitting around a City Block

If you decide to knit around your own neighborhood block, you can approach it in much the same way you'd plan a scarf. You'll need to begin by making some decisions about how wide the cowl should be, as well as its circumference. Cowls come in a wide range of sizes. For instance, it could be as large as 40 inches around, so that you can drape it around your shoulders like a shawl. Or it could be more like a neck warmer, at 20 to 25 inches around. Decide what style you prefer, then count the number of houses around your block and divide your chosen circumference by the number of houses. The result is the length in inches you'll knit for each house. Be sure to allow for knitting a few rows for each of the gray "corners"; those rows may add 3 or 4 inches to the total circumference. The width is also up to you. Cowls are usually between 8 and 13 inches wide. Cast on the number of stitches needed to achieve the measurement you choose for the width, depending on the needle size and yarn weight you choose. (For a simple ribbed cowl pattern, see page 155.)

As you knit, feel free to vary how long you knit each house, making some slightly smaller and others larger than the average, just like the real ones. My block has a large commercial building on one corner, so I will be knitting in red for many rows and putting the gray corner ridge right in the middle of all that red.

House Paint

Before you begin, you might want to decide whether you want exact color matches for the houses on your block, or if you would prefer color approximations. If a rough match will do, you might be able to make this entire project with yarn from your yarn stash. Sometimes it can be difficult to find the right color yarn that is also the right gauge. If you find a lighter-weight yarn in the right color, you might be able to double (or triple) it to match the gauge of the other knit houses. Or, if you want to take a little creative license and have more control over the colors, simply choose one lovely blue that you will use for all the blue houses, one complementary green shade for all the houses that are green, and so on. If you are a purist, try to match the colors exactly. You could even create new shades by blending multiple strands, as long as you maintain a consistent gauge.

Knock, Knock (or Not)

- You are likely to find that sometimes you need to make multiple attempts at a residence before successfully meeting its inhabitant and adding its house color to your cowl. To keep things moving and not get too discouraged, implement the following rule: After

three failed attempts to meet the inhabitants of a particular house, give yourself permission to knit that house onto your cowl without having conversed with them. Then carry on!

- If chatting with a stranger while knitting her house feels too ambitious, try simply knocking on her door after you have completed her section. Briefly say hello, exchange names, and show her the house on your cowl. Then move on. Knit the next house, and repeat.

- Lastly, it's also okay to knit around the block without knocking on your neighbors' doors at all. If this approach is more your cup of tea, just match the colors as you go. Perhaps at some point you will meet a neighbor while wearing the cowl and you can point out his house on it.

a fine PAIR

EVERY WEDDING I HAVE ATTENDED has been a whirlwind. Even with months of careful planning, weddings always seem to come together just in the nick of time. At one such recent wedding, it became clear that no one would know where to sit for dinner; we had assigned seats, but the tables weren't numbered. I made a mad dash across the garden in search of a quick solution. I picked some lavender and frantically arranged the blossoms into the shape of a different number on each table. Thankfully, this sort of thing is always part of the fun, and things rarely go sideways for very long. The love in the air can easily make up for any details that go awry: a misspoken line, a ring that is a little too tight, an unexpected downpour. And then — kiss, toast, and dance — it is suddenly over. It's time to break down the tables and return the flatware. The petals scattered down the aisle are already starting to dry, drift off, and change color. But in my mind, the ephemeral quality of the day adds immensely to its beauty.

Be an Undercover Color Collector

Such an exceptional day is certainly worthy of a gorgeous gown and perfectly tailored tux, even if only worn once ever. At the same time, I wish couples could get more mileage out of their wedding

ensembles, or at least the memory of them. Since wearing the real thing out for coffee or a concert would likely attract more attention and fuss than most of us are looking for, why not simply make a sweet handknit P.S. to the real thing?

Craft wearable wedding gifts that echo the wedding color theme by knitting striped hand warmers for the bride and a necktie for the groom.

This wedding gift of hand warmers and tie is essentially the knitter's version of pressing flowers into a scrapbook or diary. For you (aka the Undercover Color Collector), it provides a little activity to keep you entertained at the wedding. Perhaps it is a welcome relief from awkward conversations with strangers. Your task? To notice and document the most important colors of the day. It might be simple; you might decide to just snap a few good photos of the bride's bouquet or flower arrangements on the tables. Or you might want to include the linens, the scenery, and the landscape. This is where your own artistic judgment comes in. Whichever way you go about it — taking photographs on your phone or pulling

colored pencils out of your purse — you will take your findings with you to the store and find yarn to match.

Officially, we have a year to give a wedding gift, so it's okay to start knitting this pair of memory garments after the wedding. When they are done and gifted, wearing them is an opportunity for the bride and groom to remember that every day is a chance to keep saying "I do" again and again. They will get some of the fun of wearing the gown and tux, but without all the hoopla. It is a little secret for them to enjoy, perhaps on an anniversary picnic in the park.

Make a Fine Pair

The yarn choice should be a good one for both a necktie and hand warmers because you'll want to use the same skeins for them. I recommend a fine, soft wool, maybe even laceweight if you enjoy knitting on size US 0 or 1 needles. While chunky yarn makes great hand warmers, it might result in a tie that looks too silly for the groom. A finer yarn will make a lovely little ensemble that's just fancy enough to feel special. (For a pattern for hand warmers, see page 151; for a tie, see page 157.)

PINS and needles

SOMETIMES I GET AN IDEA IN MY HEAD. In this particular case, the idea was to try knitting with sewing thread on sewing pins. It seemed like something fit for a circus, perhaps right after the strongman routine. To my surprise, I managed to clumsily cast 16 stitches onto the shaft of a long glass-head pin. My fingers felt huge! After a couple of hours, I had made a teeny-tiny swatch, just about the right size and weight to be a blanket for a ladybug. Each stitch was the size of a pinprick. The gauge proved to be no fewer than 30 stitches per inch (and about 100 rows per inch). The entire "blanket" measured only ½ inch wide. If you are ever serious about handknitting a T-shirt, this would absolutely be the authentic gauge. I decided to stop when my world's smallest swatch was about 2 inches long, enough to be a sweet little finger ring. For the sake of your own sanity, I recommend you do the same. Even a ring might have more miniscule stitches than you care to make!

Challenge yourself to knit a ring using mini stitches on sewing pins with fine thread.

An Amazing Feat of Dexterity

Knit on the longest sewing pins you can find, so there is as much pin shaft as possible to grab onto with your fingertips. Begin by casting on 5 to 20 stitches, depending on how wide a ring you want to make. Garter stitch makes a wonderful, finely textured result. At the end, when you bind off, leave a 6-inch tail to sew the ends of the little strip together into a ring shape. Weave in both the beginning and ending tails to hide them. (For garter stitch, see page 136; for joining the pieces, see pages 141–143.)

Small Miracles

Each successfully knit stitch is a small miracle. In fact, it is such a delicate procedure that you might want to hold your breath for the part where you pull the new stitch through the old loop. Just remember to breathe between stitches!

Don't Look Back

I am sorry to say that if you drop a stitch, picking it back up will likely prove impossible. Feel free to chase it with the point of a pin if you like — if you can even see it — but try not to take it personally if that speck of a stitch becomes a lost cause. Push ahead!

Give Yourself a Break

If you want to take a break, keep your knitting from slipping off the pin by sticking it into a pincushion for safekeeping.

Make It Even More Special

- Alternate colors every 2 rows for a striped ring.
- Make handknit wedding rings for yourself or for a dear friend or family member.

wabi SABI

I F YOU ARE A KNITTER LIKE ME, you have probably dropped your fair
share of stitches. I'm guessing you have also unraveled whole sections
of in-process projects, watching five hours of careful knitting disappear
in just five minutes of brute yarn pulling. It's likely there are hidden
"mistakes" in your finished garments, ones that you hope no one besides
you will ever notice. You might have even had a good cry or two over all
these things.

I used to be a perfectionist, and I'm not talking just about knitting. I
thought doing good work was about getting everything just right before
sharing it with the world. Then I fell in love with Japanese teacups,
the wheel-thrown ones that are a little off-center, a bit imbalanced,

and slightly askew — in other words, a little wabi
sabi. Part of their beauty is their humility. Those
teacups are not afraid to be real, to be their honest, imperfect selves. If I could follow their lead,
perhaps I could find my own beautifully imperfect way to be. I was already imperfect; everyone
is. That part was easy. The tricky part is accepting
that fact and then embracing it. The process is
trying, but it does come with some serious perks.

For me, having integrity is about being whole. It
means that all aspects of my life — to the best of
my ability — should be infused with my values. So
in this case, I ask myself what it might mean to
knit like a Japanese teacup. What way of knitting

might mirror my desire to be honest and real, not only with myself but also with others? I think the answer here is to knit with transparency — to take risks, make mistakes, and embrace those mistakes aesthetically.

Choose a knitting project that is on the edge of your technical comfort zone. Whenever you make a mistake, instead of hiding your imperfect knitting skills, embellish them.

Honoring Imperfection, Knitwise

Embellishing my errors doesn't mean that I'll leave all the mistakes and create a grotesque, ill-fitting garment. Instead, I'll fix each mistake just enough to keep everything from going south, and then I'll commemorate the imperfection by knitting one thin stripe in another color that I have designated solely for this purpose. My imperfect nature will form a pattern across the finished garment.

When done, I can wear it as a reminder to be real, to embrace and expose my whole imperfect self. Here is where the perks come in. Not only is self-acceptance a huge relief, but it also gives us the courage to take on our most passionate, important work, even knowing that we might fail. And this gives others permission to do the same. Being real with people is absolutely essential for true connection and empathy. Each of us is a lump of clay wobbling on a pottery wheel.

On the Edge

Be sure to choose a project that's on the edge, or just outside, of your comfort zone. If you can knit a perfect pair of socks with your eyes closed, consider multicolored cabled socks instead! It's important that the project is enough of a technical challenge that you are guaranteed to mess up at least every once in a while.

Motifs of Imperfection

The thin stripe that represents a knitting imperfection can easily be swapped out for another design element: a bobble (page 138) or a purl ridge, for instance. It can also be done with more or less subtlety by using colors with more or less contrast to the predominant project colors.

out on a LIMB

LOOK AROUND YOUR NEIGHBORHOOD or town and try to imagine what it would be like if every single tree suddenly disappeared: poof! It's hard to envision, and I expect that most of us don't realize just how much we would miss them — their beautiful trunks, leaves, blossoms, and birds. It seems so natural that trees line our streets and parks, while in fact most of our city and suburban trees were planted generations ago by men and women with quite a bit of foresight. Adding just one thin growth ring per year, these trees are largely gifts from the past. Thankfully, there is a particular time of year when many trees demand our attention with a spectacular display of color-changing extravagance. The leaves burst into flaming color and then let go of their limbs and dance to the ground as if it were a blank canvas. Whether we treat raking them up into big piles as a chore or a joy is up to us.

Knit yourself fall-colored hand warmers and join the process of the changing autumn leaves.

This project's garment is its own color-changing spectacle. Even if making four pairs of hand warmers for yourself seems extravagant, that is precisely what is called for in this pattern. When you are finished, you will have a selection of hand warmers that match the colors of fall — yellow, orange, red, and brown — as if each one were a leaf. We'll never compete with the prolific range of color that nature offers, but we can knit our own small gesture, a colorful curtsy to fall. As the leaves in your neighborhood change color, be they maple, birch, or dogwood, you can wear the particular pair of warmers that mimic their changing hues. You can even choose just one particular tree to keep an eye on.

Leafing Out
You'll find a simple pattern for hand
warmers on page 151. You can work
them in simple stockinette or, for a
fancier version, use Textured Chevron
Stitch (page 140) to create a V-like texture that echoes the veins of a leaf.

Plein Air Knitting

Since real live trees inspire this project, it is best to knit these wrist warmers in the field, in the physical presence of bark and branches. Before winter sets in, find a beautiful tree and knit while sitting on the ground and leaning against its trunk. If you're inclined toward tree climbing, you could even knit while sitting up in the branches with your feet dangling down! When it becomes too chilly for your fingers, it's time to move inside, make some tea, and knit next to a tree-filled window.

How to Knit Up in a Tree

It can be helpful to rig up a basket in the tree to hold your yarn while you knit; otherwise, you are bound to climb down the tree again and again to retrieve it whenever it falls. Choose a basket with a handle and simply tie it onto the same branch you are sitting on. Set your ball of yarn in the basket and let it dangle just below you. The ball will simply unroll in the basket as you pull the yarn up into your lap for knitting.

Add to the Ensemble

You might also want to knit leg warmers to go with the hand warmers: brown, round as a trunk, and with a bark-like stitch pattern. Just like tree bark, these leg warmers will mark the boundary between you and the outside world, protecting you from it, but also connecting you to it. Being able to stay warm lets us enjoy cold-weather outings, be they skipping through piles of leaves, catching snowflakes on our tongues, or scurrying over to a friend's house. For a simple leg-warmer pattern, see pages 151–152. Stitch patterns with bark-like textures include Diagonal Rib (page 140), Seeded Rib (page 137), and Double Moss (page 138).

dormitory HOP

I AM TERRIBLE AT SMALL TALK. I always have been. It makes me want to leave the party, run home, and hide under my bed just in case anyone followed me. If I were the bold conversationalist that I sometimes wish I were instead of the introvert that I am, I would just ask strangers what I really want to know: "What is the most important thing to you in the world?" or "What is the saddest thing you have ever witnessed?" or "What gives you hope?" Oh, how I wish someone would ask me questions like these while shaking my hand for the first time!

I met a lot of new people when I went off to college. On the first day of my first year, I arrived at my big brick dormitory with a giant duffel bag full of clothes, keepsakes, and an array of knitting needles. Suddenly being surrounded by fresh faces was exciting — and intimidating.

Hiding under my bed and knitting was not an option. My bed was inconveniently located in the midst of hundreds of other beds and everyone would find out, including the boys in the room above mine who liked to dangle vacuum cleaners out the window by the cord. If I could travel back in time and give 18-year-old me a tip, I would whisper this project idea into my own ear. It is not necessarily easier than small talk, for it is awkward in its own ways, but it does promise to be more lively and rewarding.

Start a Scarf, Start a Conversation

I wish I had picked some yarns back then, assigned each ball a deep get-to-know-you question, and hopped down the dorm hall, ducking into room after room, knitting a simple scarf and chatting along the way. I would knock on each half-open door and say something like "Will you help me with my scarf by answering a Deep Question?" I would point to each color of yarn and explain which question goes with it, almost like a menu. "Take your pick, and I'll knit while we talk. I will add a stripe to my scarf that corresponds to the color of the question you answer. I promise to answer it, too." And I would continue so on, down the entire hall, until I had a complete scarf. Or I'd at least go until I met a really neat boy.

Knitting this scarf can lead to great conversations. The delightful structure of the project inspires everyone involved to open up and share something real.

Deep Questions

When you make your list of Deep Questions, include options for various comfort levels. There should be at least one fallback question that anyone would be comfortable answering. If the rest of your questions are too much for them, they can at least, for example, tell you about their favorite book. Here are some questions you could ask:

- What was your favorite childhood toy? Tell me why you loved it.

- What is one thing you know for sure is true about love?

- Tell me about a time when you were lost, and a time when you were found.

- What is the bravest thing you have ever done?

- What's the most recent work of art that you got really excited about?

- Would you want to live forever if you could choose to?

- What animal, plant, or color do you identify with, and why?

- Tell me about something that drives you crazy.

- What gives you hope?

- What is your favorite book and why?

Practical Concerns

- Here is a tidy way to visually represent the color/question choices to your conversationalists. Put each ball of yarn into its own small cardboard box (or tissue box), write the question on the outside of the box, and punch a hole to thread the yarn through. This will make it easy for your conversation partner to see his or her options. You then simply draw the yarn from the box they choose.
- Make a garment that is easy for you to work on while you talk, one that does not require much concentration: a scarf, leg warmers, or a cowl, for instance. If you can knit socks with your eyes closed and without puzzling your way through a paper pattern, feel free!

Not Just for College Students

If you are not a college student, you can still make a Deep Questions item using color-coded questions. Perhaps set up café dates with your friends and present the questions to them over a pot of tea.

party POPPER

SERIOUS KNITTERS HAVE A REPUTATION for accumulating baskets, boxes, and even closets full of yarn. Whether they are leftovers, lost causes, or the next 10 batters up, the twisted skeins and hand-rolled balls seem to multiply on their own when we're not looking. One reason for our stash's steady swell is that it's possible to stumble upon a particular gorgeous yarn exactly once and never again. We must buy it while we can, because rare yarns are beautiful creatures that can go extinct. But each tiny mission to rescue another endangered species of yarn only adds to the size of our

beloved stash. At some point, however, it simply becomes ridiculous. Yet we go on a little more, until finally we can pile it no higher. This is the perfect moment to organize a yarn swap or donate a batch to a thrift store. And while you're at it, here's a way to make it festive.

Before giving away your surplus yarn, collect little surprises and hide them in the centers of the balls.

Hidden Treasures

For example, obtain a tiny plastic dinosaur and make a new ball of yarn by rewrapping the original ball around the toy. When some future knitter eventually works his way to the center of the ball, he will be pleasantly surprised by a little treat! Some other appropriate treats might be a little bouncy ball, a beautiful seashell, or a silver dollar. I would avoid perishables since it could be decades before your surprises are revealed! A 10-year-old peppermint just won't do. But a bubble wand, a spinning top, or a swirly glass marble would be delightful.

with hands JUST SO

I ADMIT IT. A ball winder is a beautiful tool. It is a master of its task. I have one. And yet, I know for a fact that my dad as a youth held skeins of yarn for his mother while she wound them into balls by hand. I love the image of the two of them connected by a thin string, conversing as the skein between his palms slowly transformed into a ball between hers. The beauty of it is that she had him cornered. When I picture my dad — age 10, age 12, age 16 — sweetly holding skeins for my grandmother while she chatted away, the ball winder suddenly seems a very lonely object.

Next time you have some skeins to turn into balls, leave your ball winder in the closet.

Instead of using a ball winder, find a friend and ask him to kindly hold his hands just so: about 2 feet apart, fingers together and thumbs up. Get creative about whom you ask. It might be a friend with whom you want to catch up. Or maybe it's a stranger on a park bench. If you have multiple skeins to wind, you could set out to wind each one with a different stranger in the park. Or you could use this as an opportunity to get to know your next-door neighbor better, winding the skeins together on her front stoop.

how to invent your own project

Are you curious to design your own project in the spirit of this book? Perhaps you already have a spark of an idea: a gift occasion, a milestone event, a topic to explore, data to document, a new habit to practice, even just a lovely skein of yarn in an incredible color? Anything in life that is special or important can become the perfect seed for one of these knitting projects. Walk with me through the next few pages as I sketch out a design process to help you develop your own idea. Sometimes creativity is tidy; usually it is not. Follow the steps below, or incorporate bits and pieces of the steps into whatever creative process works for you!

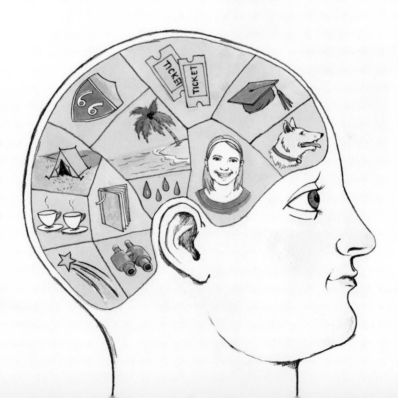

Step 1: Choose an Idea

This is the heart and soul of this way of knitting. You will need an idea, something wonderful and awesome and heartfelt. For now, it can be abstract or concrete. The idea should be one you're excited to spend some time with. It might be one of the following:

- a person
- a place
- a creature
- a thing
- a big life event
- an everyday experience
- an emotion
- a memory
- a problem to solve
- a curiosity
- a journey
- a work of art (such as a book, song, film, painting, and so on)

Step 2: Gather Details

Beauty is in the details when it comes to this way of knitting. Once you've chosen an idea, find some notepaper and write your idea nice and big at the top. Then fill the page with details that go with your idea. This should be a big wild brainstorm — the more the better. Let yourself go off on tangents. Follow your instincts and curiosities. Let yourself get really specific whenever you're inspired to. Dig up details by doing online research. Whatever generates relevant content is fair game! Perhaps do the following along the way:

- Describe the scene.
- Add sensory details: sight, scent, sound, touch, taste.
- Explore: what, where, when, who, how, why?
- Tell the story.
- Write about what it feels like emotionally.
- Try to figure out what it means, and what it is all about in a bigger sense.

After you've got a nice big brainstorm and a page or two full of notes, then go back and highlight the most interesting, meaningful, important details — the ones you want to work with in your project. You might not be able to work in all of them, but go ahead and carry your favorite parts into step 3.

Step 3: Translate

The next step is to translate your idea, with some of its marvelous details, into a knitted object. Paying equal attention to aesthetics and process provides many creative opportunities to further embed the garment with your idea and make it a remarkably meaningful object. The considerations below are not all equally relevant for every idea, so let your particular idea guide you to the considerations that make the most sense for your project. Keeping in mind your favorite highlighted ideas from step 2, jot down notes in response to aesthetics as well as process.

AESTHETICS

Think about the potential meanings of physical phenomena (colors, shapes, textures, and so on) and how they tie back into your main idea or theme.

- *Shape/form:* What type of garment or other object? Is it useful? Decorative? What size in terms of general heft and presence? (Large, like an ocean? Small as a bird?) What construction method?

- *Color:* Which colors? (White for the moon?) How much color variety? (One for each mood? Each person? Each book?) How many? What hues? (Like fall leaves?)

- *Texture:* What yarn weight? What type of fiber or feel? What needle size or gauge? (Big needles, for a whale?) How heavy- or lightweight? (Light, like a rose petal?) What stitch patterns? (Seed Stitch for a gardener? Honeycomb for a beekeeper?)

PROCESS

Think about the entire life of the object — from what it looks like to how it is made to how it is eventually enjoyed — and how those activities tie back in to your main idea or theme.

Preparing. Where does the yarn come from? How is it obtained? (Purchased on a special trip? From your great-grandmother's stash?) What is the source of the needles or other tools? (Do you knit it on hand-whittled twigs from the forest? Do you dye the yarn with native plants?)

Making. Where will you make it? (On the subway? Up in a tree? On a park bench?) What determines each stitch? Is each stitch, stripe, or bobble in response to a particular event or activity? (A home run? A laugh?) When or why do you switch colors, textures, shapes, and so on? What is the overall timeline of making? (A day? A year? A century?) How fast or how slow, and why?

Enjoying. Who wears or uses the finished item? (Your best friend? A child?) When and where is it worn? For a specific circumstance, moment, or place? How is it worn? (On an anniversary? On a boat?) Can it be worn different ways for different reasons? (Is it reversible — one color for daytime, another for nighttime?)

Step 4: Bring It Together

To finalize a design, next I generally browse all of my notes (or go for a walk in a park) until something clicks and — voilà! Sometimes it's instant and obvious; other times I need to return to previous steps and keep working on it. I might need to interview someone, or do a little more research to flesh out an important detail, or even just sleep on it. The main activity of step 4 is reviewing all of your notes so far with the goal of drawing together a handful of details, aesthetic qualities, and experiential processes into a meaningful project that is wonderfully personal. A strong project will have good reasons behind each design decision — reasons that connect back to the beautiful idea you began with. Good luck, and I can't wait to see what you dream up!

R.S.V.P.

I hope this book has sparked some new ideas for you, and perhaps even put a skip in your step between reading sessions. Next time you are ready for a new knitting project, I invite you to take the long way to the knitting shop. I encourage you to see what happens when you let knitting connect you in playful, wildly creative ways with the broader world — with the people and places you love. Let the adventure that is your life — hiking in the woods, attending a wedding, reading a favorite book, having tea with your best friend — find its way into your stitches and imbue them with great beauty.

APPENDIX

pattern stitches

Stockinette Stitch

- **ROWS:** Knit 1 row, purl 1 row alternately when working back and forth on straight needles.

- **ROUNDS:** Knit every round when working in the round on circular or double-pointed needles.

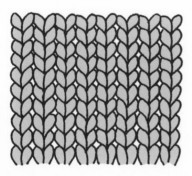

Garter Stitch

- **ROWS:** Knit every row when working back and forth on straight needles.

- **ROUNDS:** Knit 1 round, purl 1 round alternately when working in the round on circular or double-pointed needles.

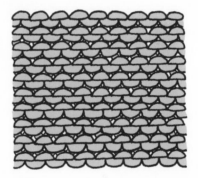

Seed Stitch

The stitch has a bumpy texture — like a sprinkling of seeds! Be sure to work this stitch pattern on an uneven number of stitches. *Note:* You will always knit into a purl stitch and purl into a knit stitch, whether you're working on the right or wrong side of the fabric.

- **ALL ROWS**: P1, *K1, P1; repeat from * across every row.

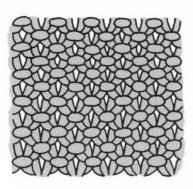

Seeded Rib

To work this pattern for Seeded Rib, your stitch count needs to be a multiple of 4, plus 3.

ROW 1: K3, *P1, K3; repeat from * to end of row.

ROW 2: K1, *P1, K3; repeat from * until 2 stitches remain, then P1, K1.

Repeat these 2 rows as long as you'd like!

Bobbles

STEP 1. At the place where you want a bobble, knit into the front, into the back, and again into the front of the next stitch before letting the original stitch slide off the needle.

STEP 2. Don't continue knitting. Instead, turn the needle and purl the 3 stitches you made in step 1. Stop again, and turn back to the right side.

STEP 3. Slip the first 2 stitches, knit the next stitch (the 3rd in your cluster from step 1), then pass the slipped stitches together over the knit stitch. You are now back to just 1 stitch, and you have a little puff in its place. Continue along and finish the row (or round).

VARIATIONS

- For the decrease in step 3, simply knit the 3 stitches together. Experiment; you'll get a slightly different look depending on how you do it.

- Instead of making the decrease in step 3, knit the 3 stitches, turn and purl the 3 stitches, then turn and execute the step 3 decrease. This will give you a bigger bobble.

- For larger bobbles, you can also make 5, 7, or even 9 stitches in the original stitch.

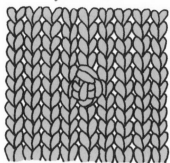

finished bobble

Double Moss Stitch

Your stitch count needs to be a multiple of 4 to work this pattern.

ROWS 1 AND 2: *K2, P2; repeat from * to end of row.

ROWS 3 AND 4: *P2, K2: repeat from * to end of row.

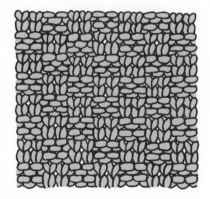

Basketweave Stitch

This pattern for Basketweave Stitch is written to be knit in the round on circular or double-pointed needles. Your stitch count needs to be a multiple of 8.

ROUND 1: Knit all the way around.

ROUNDS 2–6: *K4, P4; repeat from * to end of round.

ROUND 7: Knit all the way around.

ROUNDS 8–12: *P4, K4; repeat from * to end of round.

Repeat rounds 1–12.

Raspberry Stitch

This pattern for Raspberry Stitch is written to be worked in the round on circular or double-pointed needles. Your stitch count needs to be a multiple of 4. Notice that the wrong side of the fabric is facing you as you work this stitch. When you're finished knitting, turn the piece inside out and admire the textured "berries"!

ROUNDS 1 AND 3: Knit all the way around.

ROUND 2: *(K1, P1, K1) into next stitch, p3tog; repeat from * to end of round.

ROUND 4: *P3tog, (K1, P1, K1) into next stitch; repeat from * to end of round.

Repeat these 4 rows for the pattern.

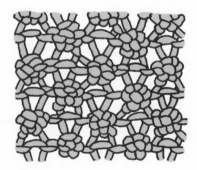

Diagonal Rib

This pattern for Diagonal Rib is written to be worked in the round on circular or double-pointed needles. Your stitch count needs to be a multiple of 4.

ROUNDS 1 AND 2: *K2, P2; repeat from * to end of round.

ROUNDS 3 AND 4: K1, *P2, K2; repeat from * until 3 stitches remain, then P2, K1.

ROUNDS 5 AND 6: * P2, K2; repeat from * to end of round.

ROUNDS 7 AND 8: P1, *K2, P2; repeat from * until 3 stitches remain, K2, P1.

Repeat rounds 1–8 for pattern.

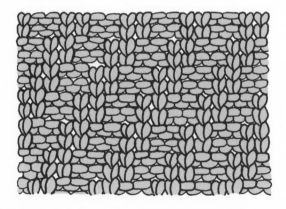

Textured Chevron Stitch

This pattern for Textured Chevron Stitch is written to be worked in the round on double-pointed or circular needles. Your stitch count needs to be a multiple of 15. This stitch will be easier to work if you arrange your stitches so that the yarnovers do not fall at the ends of the needles.

ROUND 1: *K1, yo, K5, ssk, k2tog, K5, yo; repeat from * to end of round.

ROUND 2: Purl.

Repeat rounds 1–2 for pattern.

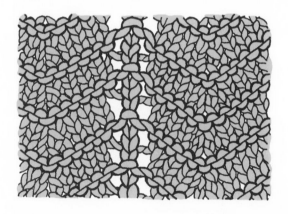

Managing Multiple Yarns

- When you work stripes using two or more yarns, it's important always to add 2 rows of any one color at a time. This is so that you return yarns to the edge where you began them, ready to use when you need them again. To keep all colors available at any given time, you must carry all the strands up the edge of the piece along the way. To do this, take the yarn you are about to knit a row with and wrap it around the unused strands before you start the new row. Always wrap around in the same direction so you get a nice twist pattern up the edge.

- Choose a permanent place in your home to keep your project to prevent the yarns from getting all tangled up in your bag. Before knitting each row, arrange the balls to sort out any twists that have developed.

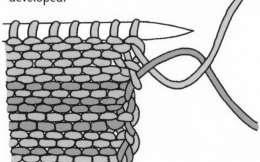

Joining Knit Pieces Together

We knitters have many choices for how to seam our knitting. Before you attach the pieces, however, be sure to block them by pinning them to foam or another material you can push pins into. They'll be much easier to match up and join if the edges are smooth and straight. Before pinning, you can first immerse the pieces in water and roll them up in a terry-cloth towel to remove excess water, or you can dampen the pieces by lightly spraying them with water after you've pinned them out. As you pin them down, measure the sides of each piece and adjust them as needed, so that they match and align properly with their neighbors when you start assembling them. Let them dry thoroughly before seaming. Here are three of the most common ways of seaming knitted pieces together.

MATTRESS STITCH

STEP 1. Lay the pieces to be joined side by side, right side up. Thread a tapestry needle with the same yarn you used to knit the pieces.

STEP 2. Insert your needle into the middle of an edge stitch on one piece, go under one horizontal strand, and then pull the yarn through.

(continued on next page)

(Mattress Stitch, continued)

STEP 3. Insert your needle in the middle of an edge stitch in the next row opposite where you came up, and go under one strand, pulling the yarn through in the same way.

Continue to zigzag from side to side, moving up along the edges. Pull the yarn through gently as you stitch so that the knitting is drawn together, creating an almost invisible seam on the right side.

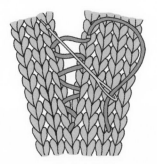

CROCHET JOIN

You may work this join on either the right or wrong side of a fabric, depending on which look you prefer. When you work with the right sides of the pieces against each other, as described below, the seam will show on the wrong side of the fabric. If you place wrong sides against each other as you stitch, the seam will show on the right side of the fabric, creating a decorative ridge.

STEP 1. Hold the two pieces you are joining so that their right sides are against each other and their edges are aligned. Select a yarn in matching or contrasting color and an appropriate-sized hook.

STEP 2. Single crochet through both loops of an edge stitch on each piece. (You will be inserting your hook under 4 loops, then working a normal single crochet stitch.)

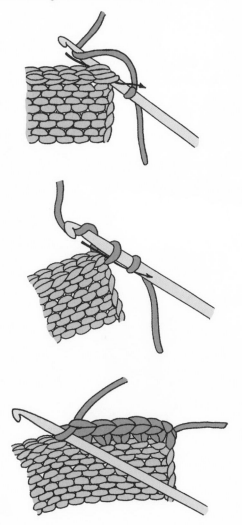

KITCHENER STITCH

Kitchener Stitch (also called "grafting") is another way to join two pieces of knitted fabric. It is done on "live" stitches, before binding off. To set up for it, place half the stitches on one needle and the other half on another needle. Arrange the needles with their points facing in the same direction and with the wrong sides of the fabric facing each other. Thread a piece of project yarn through a tapestry needle. (Plan ahead and cut a long tail at the end of one of the pieces you are joining.)

STEP 1. Insert the tapestry needle into the first stitch on the front needle as if you were going to knit with it. Draw the yarn through the stitch, and slip it off the needle.

STEP 2. Insert the needle through the next stitch on the front needle from right to left (as if you were going to purl it), draw the yarn through, but leave the stitch on the needle.

STEP 3. Insert the needle through the first stitch on the back needle as if you were going to purl it. Draw the yarn through the stitch, and slip it off the needle.

STEP 4. Insert the needle through the next stitch on the back needle as if you were going to knit it. Draw the yarn through the stitch, but leave the stitch on the needle.

Repeat steps 1–4 until all of the stitches have been joined. Draw the yarn through the remaining stitch and fasten off.

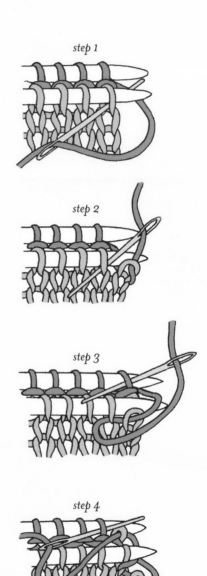

step 1

step 2

step 3

step 4

Picking Up Stitches

Use this technique to pick up stitches along a bound-off, cast-on, or side edge, so that you have new live stitches on a needle ready to knit a new section.

STEP 1. With the right side of the piece facing you, insert the knitting needle under both strands of an edge stitch.

STEP 2. Wrap the yarn around the needle and knit a new stitch through the edge stitch.

picking up stitches on a bound-off edge

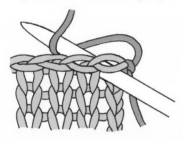

picking up stitches on a side edge

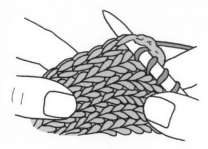

Picot Bind Off

STEP 1. K2, then bind off 1 stitch.

STEP 2. Turn the needle with the remaining stitch and cast on 3. (You can use the Backward-Loop Cast On, opposite, to do this.) You will have 4 stitches on this needle.

STEP 3. Turn the needle again, and draw the second, third, and fourth stitches over the first stitch on the right-hand needle.

STEP 4. Bind off 2 stitches.

Repeat steps 2–4 until you have 1 stitch. Cut the yarn, and draw the tail through the remaining stitch to fasten off.

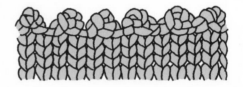

A Knitted Slit

These directions for a slit can be adjusted to make a slit small enough for a buttonhole or large enough to tuck the end of a scarf through.

STEP 1. Work to the spot where you want your slit to begin.

STEP 2. Bind off enough stitches so that the bound-off edge measures the length you want for your slit, then continue working your pattern until the end of the row.

STEP 3. Turn and work back across the row until you reach the point where you bound off. Using the Backward-Loop Cast On at right, cast on the number of stitches you bound off in the previous row, *then cast on 1 extra stitch.* Complete the row by working the remaining stitches in your pattern stitch.

STEP 4. Turn and on the next row work to the cast-on stitches. Work all but one of the cast-on stitches, then knit the last cast-on stitch together with the next stitch: knitting these 2 stitches together helps avoid the little hole that often appears between the last cast-on stitch and the remainder of the row. You now should be back to the original stitch count.

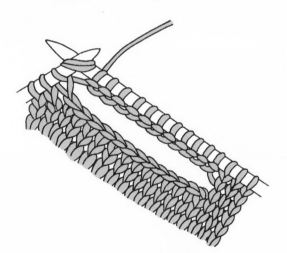

Backward-Loop Cast On

You can use this method of casting on in a variety of situations, but it's especially useful when you need to cast on in the middle of a row or at the end of a row.

STEP 1. Hold the needle that will receive the cast-on stitches in your right hand. (You use only one needle for this cast on.)

STEP 2. Wrap the yarn counterclockwise around your left forefinger or thumb so that it creates a loop with the working end over the end that's attached to the stitches already on the needle.

STEP 3. Insert the needle through the loop as though you were knitting and slide the loop onto the needle.

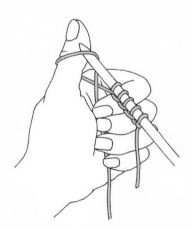

Whipstitch

This basic stitch has many uses, both decorative and practical. If you are joining two pieces of knitting, place them against each other with right sides facing if you want to hide the seam, or wrong sides facing if you want the seam to serve as a decorative element on the outside of your project.

STEP 1. Insert the needle into the back of the knitting and draw the thread through.

STEP 2. Allowing the yarn to wrap over the edge of the knitting, again insert the needle through the back a short distance away from your first stitch.

Continue in this way, making stitches a consistent distance apart as well as a consistent distance from the fabric edge.

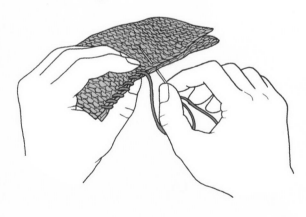

Adding Beads to Your Knitting

For this method of adding beads to your knitting, you'll need a crochet hook small enough to fit through the holes in the beads you want to use. When you come to the stitch where you want to place a bead, here's how to do it:

STEP 1. Insert your hook through the bead and then into the next stitch on the left needle.

STEP 2. Draw the stitch through the hole in the bead, then replace the stitch on the left needle.

STEP 3. Knit the stitch as usual.

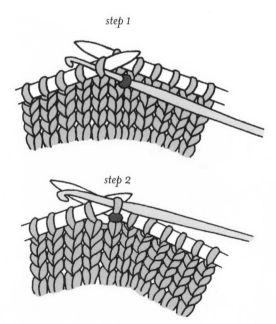

step 1

step 2

Simple Socks

This basic sock pattern is written for two sizes: woman's medium and (with stitch numbers and measurements in parentheses) man's medium. It uses sport-weight yarn worked on four size US 3 (3.25 mm) double-pointed needles to get a gauge of 6 stitches to an inch in stockinette stitch. (Take time to make a swatch to be sure you are getting the correct gauge. Not all sport-weight yarn will give you this gauge with this size needle, so you may need to use a smaller or larger needle to ensure that your sock will come out to the right measurement. If you use a stitch pattern other than stockinette, work your gauge swatch in the stitch pattern you plan to use for the sock.)

SETUP

Cast on 48 (56) stitches. Divide the stitches among three double-pointed needles as follows:

- Needle 1: 12 (14) stitches

- Needle 2: 24 (28) stitches

- Needle 3: 12 (14) stitches

Use the yarn from the last cast-on stitch to knit the first cast-on stitch. This joins the stitches so that you can begin knitting in a round. Take care not to twist any of the stitches as you do so.

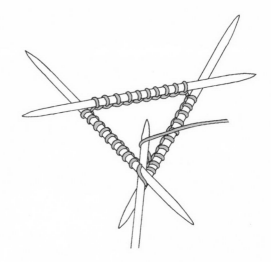

KNITTING THE SOCKS

ROUNDS 1–8 (RIBBING): *K1, P1; repeat from * to the end of each round.

NEXT ROUNDS (LEG): Knit every round if you work stockinette stitch. If you wish, work one of the stitch patterns on pages 136–140 or from a favorite stitch dictionary, or change colors to make stripes, as for the *Sweet Possibilities* (page 22) or *Brave Stitches* (page 102) socks. Work until the sock measures 6" (8") from the cast-on edge (including the ribbing).

CREATING THE HEEL FLAP

SETUP: Knit across Needles 1 and 2. Set the 24 (28) Needle 2 stitches just knit on a stitch holder. Knit Needle 3 stitches and then Needle 1 stitches onto one needle. Work on only these 24 (28) stitches for heel flap. Purl 1 row.

(continued on next page)

(Simple Socks, continued)

ROW 1: *Slip 1 purlwise with the yarn in back, K1; repeat from * to the end of the row.

ROW 2: Slip 1 purlwise with the yarn in front, purl to the end of the row.

Repeat rows 1 and 2 twelve (fourteen) more times, then knit row 1 once more; the heel flap will measure about 2½" (2¾"). [You will have worked 27 (31) rows in all.]

SHAPING THE HEEL

ROW 1 (WRONG SIDE): Slip 1, P12 (14), p2tog, P1, turn [leave 8 (10) stitches unknit].

ROW 2: Slip 1, K3, ssk, K1, turn [leave 8 (10) stitches unknit].

ROW 3: Slip 1, P4, p2tog, P1, turn [leave 6 (8) stitches unknit].

ROW 4: Slip 1, K5, ssk, K1, turn [leave 6 (8) stitches unknit].

ROW 5: Slip 1, P6, p2tog, P1, turn [leave 4 (6) stitches unknit].

ROW 6: Slip 1, K7, ssk, K1, turn [leave 4 (6) stitches unknit].

ROW 7: Slip 1, P8, p2tog, P1, turn [leave 2 (4) stitches unknit].

ROW 8: Slip 1, K9, ssk, K1, turn [leave 2 (4) stitches unknit].

ROW 9: Slip 1, P10, p2tog, P1, turn [leave 0 (2) stitches unknit].

ROW 10: Slip 1, K11, ssk, K1, turn [leave 0 (2) stitches unknit].

ROW 11 (MAN'S MEDIUM ONLY): Slip 1, P12, p2tog, P1, turn [leave 0 stitches unknit].

ROW 12 (MAN'S MEDIUM ONLY): Slip 1, K13, ssk, K1, turn [leave 0 stitches unknit].

You will have 14 (16) stitches on this needle.

WORKING THE GUSSET

- Holding your knitting so the right side of the heel flap is facing you, pick up 15 (17) stitches along the left side of the heel flap. Then pick up 1 extra stitch between the edge stitches and the stitches on the stitch holder.

- Place the 24 (28) stitches on the holder on an empty needle and knit across. This is the new Needle 2.

- With an empty needle, pick up 1 stitch in the gap between Needle 2 and the stitches at the bottom of the right side of the heel flap. Then, pick up 15 (17) stitches along the right side of the heel flap. Knit the next 7 (8) stitches onto the same needle. This is the new Needle 3.

You are now at the center of the back of the sock, and the next needle is the new Needle 1. The stitch counts are as follows:

- Needle 1: 23 (26)

- Needle 2: 24 (28)

- Needle 3: 23 (26)

Begin again to *work in the round.*

ROUND 1:

- Needle 1: Knit to the last 3 stitches, K2tog, K1.

- Needle 2: Knit to the end of the needle.

- Needle 3: K1, ssk, knit to the end of the needle.

ROUND 2: Knit to end of needle.

Repeat rounds 1 and 2 until the stitch counts on Needles 1 and 3 are reduced to 12 (14) stitches on each needle [48 (56) stitches in all].

WORKING THE FOOT

Knit every row until the piece measures 1½" (1¾") less than desired length, about 7¾" (8½") from where you picked up the heel stitches.

TOE SHAPING

ROUND 1:

- **NEEDLE 1:** Knit to the last 3 stitches, K2tog, K1.

- **NEEDLE 2:** K1, ssk, knit to the last 3 stitches, K2tog, K1.

- **NEEDLE 3:** K1, ssk, knit to the end of the row.

ROUND 2: Knit all stitches.

Repeat rounds 1 and 2 until you have 12 stitches left, divided among the needles as follows:

- **NEEDLE 1:** 3 (3) stitches

- **NEEDLE 2:** 6 (6) stitches

- **NEEDLE 3:** 3 (3) stitches

End with a round 1, then knit the 3 (3) stitches on Needle 1.

FINISHING

Place all of the stitches on Needles 1 and 3 on the same needle (6 stitches); 6 stitches remain on Needle 2. Place the needles side by side with the wrong sides of the sock facing each other. Use Kitchener Stitch to close the toe (see page 143). Weave in the ends.

Basic Hat

It's easy to custom-fit a handknit hat to any size head. To make one in worsted-weight yarn, you're going to have to do a little math — but just a little! Begin by taking two head measurements of the person who will be wearing the hat: one around the forehead and to the back of the neck (at about where the bottom edge of the hat will be) and one from where the center of the hat will fall at the crown of the head to where the bottom edge at the back will be (the nape of the neck).

Next, knit a swatch with the yarn and needles you plan to use for the hat. If you're using worsted-weight yarn, make the swatch about 25 stitches wide and knit until the swatch is just about square. (*Note:* Ideally, you should work the stitch pattern you'll be using for the hat, but the pattern is written to be knit in the round. A shortcut to doing this is to knit a small tube — about 25 stitches — about 4" long, then cut it open to get a square swatch on which you can measure the stitches per inch.) When it's complete, count how many stitches

(continued on next page)

you're getting in 4", then divide that number by 4 to find out your gauge, or how many stitches you're getting in 1". (You may wonder why you don't just count how many stitches you're getting in 1" in the first place, but you are unlikely to factor in partial stitches, and they really do matter. It's much safer and more accurate to measure over 4" and then calculate the average.) Multiply the number of stitches in 1" on your swatch by the around-the-head measurement of the hat's wearer; this gives you the total number of stitches you need to cast on. If you're knitting your hat in stockinette or garter stitch, you can skip right ahead to Setup, below, and cast on. If your pattern stitch requires that your stitch count be a multiple of a certain number (such as with Basketweave or Raspberry Stitch), there's one more consideration you need to take into account.

Look at the pattern stitches you'll use. Basketweave Stitch (page 139) requires that your total stitch count be a multiple of 8; Raspberry Stitch (page 139) requires that the total be a multiple of 4. Take your final stitch count and round it down to get a number that is the correct multiple for the pattern. (For a good fit, you usually need fewer stitches than indicated by the gauge in your swatch.) This is the number you need to cast on in order to (1) have the hat fit the wearer and (2) accommodate the stitch multiple of your pattern.

Because the hat is intended to be worked in stitch patterns that can be a little tricky to decrease for a rounded crown, I've designed it to be knit on circular needles to form a straight-sided tube. When the hat is the desired length, you simply run a length of yarn through all the stitches, pull them together, and fasten off.

SETUP

Using a 16"-long circular needle in a size suitable for your yarn, cast on the number of stitches you calculated. Use the yarn from the last cast-on stitch to knit the first cast-on stitch. This joins the stitches so that you can begin knitting in a round. Take care not to twist any of the stitches. Place a stitch marker at the beginning of the round to keep track of where each round ends and begins.

KNITTING THE HAT

ROUNDS 1–6 (RIBBING): *K1, P1; repeat from * to the end of the round. (*Note:* Consider using a needle one or two sizes smaller for the ribbing, so that the hat fits snugly around the forehead.)

NEXT ROUNDS (STITCH PATTERN): Begin working the stitch pattern (see Basketweave Stitch or Raspberry Stitch, page 139). Work the stitch pattern until the measurement from the cast-on edge (including the ribbing) is the same as the measurement from the crown to the nape of the neck. Complete a full pattern repeat before continuing to the final step.

FINISHING

Cut the yarn, leaving an 10" tail. Thread the tail through a tapestry needle and run it through all the stitches on the needle. For a more secure finish, run the yarn through a second time. Take the thread to the inside of the hat and fasten off securely. (*Note:* Unless your working yarn is very strong, you may want to reinforce it by running a stronger yarn, such as an acrylic or cotton, through the stitches when you fasten them off.)

Hand Warmers

Hand warmers are quick and fun to make, but if you're feeling more ambitious, you may prefer to knit up fingerless gloves, mittens, or even gloves with fingers. This pattern is worked with worsted-weight wool on a set of US 7 (4.5 mm) double-pointed needles to get a gauge of about 4 stitches per inch. (For the hand warmers described in *A Fine Pair* on page 111, use laceweight yarn and whatever size needles gives you a gauge of 10 stitches to an inch — probably size US 0.) Note that the abbreviation *kfb* means that you should knit into the front and then into the back of the same stitch before dropping it off the needle; this increases 1 stitch to 2.

SETUP

Loosely cast on 30 stitches (60 stitches for laceweight yarn). Use the yarn from the last cast-on stitch to knit the first cast-on stitch. This joins the stitches so that you can begin knitting in a round. Take care not to twist any of the stitches as you do so. Place a stitch marker so you can keep track of where each round begins and ends.

KNITTING THE CUFF

ROUNDS 1–8 (RIBBING): *K1, P1; repeat from * to the end of the round.

PATTERN ROUNDS

For *Out on a Limb* (page 119), work the Textured Chevron Stitch pattern (page 140) until the hand warmer, including the ribbing, measures about 6" from the cast-on edge. Finish a full pattern repeat

before proceeding to the top ribbing. Kfb in the last stitch of the final round so that you again have an even number of stitches to work the ribbing. (*Note:* You may choose other stitch patterns, if you prefer.)

TOP RIBBING

Work the same ribbing pattern you worked in rounds 1–7. Cast off loosely in the ribbing pattern.

Leg Warmers

This pattern is worked with worsted-weight wool on a set of five US 7 (4.5 mm) double-pointed needles to get a gauge of 4 stitches per inch. You may work these leg warmers in stitches other than Diagonal Rib (page 140), if you prefer.

SETUP

Loosely cast on 48 stitches. Divide the stitches evenly among four needles (12 stitches per needle). Use the yarn from the last cast-on stitch to knit the first cast-on stitch. This joins the stitches so that you can begin knitting in a round. Take care not to twist any of the stitches as you do so. Use the yarn tail to keep track of where each round begins and ends.

KNITTING THE CUFF

ROUNDS 1–7 (RIBBING): *K2, P2; repeat from * to the end of the round.

ROUND 8: *K11, kfb; repeat from * to the end of the round. You will have 52 stitches (13 stitches per needle). (*Kfb* means to increase by knitting into

(continued on next page)

(Leg Warmers, continued)

the front and then into the back of the same stitch before dropping it off the needle.)

PATTERN ROUNDS

Work the Diagonal Rib pattern (page 140) until the leg warmer measures about 12" from the cast-on edge (include the ribbing in your measurement). Finish a full repeat of the stitch pattern before proceeding to the bottom ribbing.

BOTTOM RIBBING

Work the same ribbing pattern you worked in rounds 1–7. Cast off loosely in the ribbing pattern.

Hexagon Shape

Use the following instructions to make a single coaster, or make 24 hexagons so that you can create the honeycomb purse of *Nectar Collector* (page 34); instructions are on page 154.

SETUP

I used DK-weight linen yarn in yellow and dark gold for this pattern.

Using size US 5 (3.75 mm) double-pointed needles and the yellow yarn, cast on 54 stitches. Leave a 12" tail that you can use later for sewing the hexagons together. Divide the stitches evenly among three needles (18 stitches on each). Use the yarn from the last cast-on stitch to knit the first cast-on stitch. This joins the stitches so that you can begin knitting in a round. Take care not to twist any of the stitches as you do so. It's helpful to place a stitch marker at the beginning of the round so that you can keep track of where the round begins and ends.

KNITTING THE HEXAGON

ROUND 1: Still using the yellow yarn, knit around, placing markers between the 9th and 10th stitches on each needle. The markers, along with the ends of the needles, divide the piece into six equal sections and indicate the points where you will make your decreases to the center.

ROUND 2: Change to the dark gold yarn and knit around.

ROUND 3: *K2tog, knit to 2 stitches before the marker and ssk, slip the marker, k2tog, knit to 2 stitches before the end of the needle and ssk; repeat from * to the end of the round. (42 stitches; 14 on each needle)

ROUNDS 4 AND 5: Knit.

Repeat rounds 3–5 two more times. (18 stitches; 6 on each needle)

NEXT ROUND: *K2tog around. (9 stitches; 3 on each needle)

FINISHING

Cut the yarn, leaving a 6" tail. Thread the tail through a tapestry needle and run the needle through the 9 remaining stitches. Draw them up snugly to close the center hole, then take the needle through the center to the wrong side of the hexagon, fasten it off, and weave in the end.

Use the first hexagon you knit as a template for all the others, taking care to make the measurements match as closely as possible.

BLOCKING

Immerse the hexagons in water, then roll them in a terry-cloth towel to remove the excess water. Lay them on a piece of foam or a similar surface. Pin each corner and use enough pins along the edges to get them as straight as possible, to make the hexagon shape clear, and to make them of equal size. Allow to dry thoroughly.

TO ASSEMBLE THE PURSE

Lay two hexagons together with right sides facing and one edge of each aligned with the other. Thread a length of the project yarn into a tapestry needle and use whipstitch (page 146) to join the hexagons, inserting your tapestry needle into half of an edge stitch on each side. When you have stitched together all the hexagons, weave in any remaining loose ends.

Coaster Variation

If you are making coasters instead of a purse, cast on 66 stitches, place markers between the 10th and 11th stitches, and repeat rounds 3–5 four times in all. Block when complete.

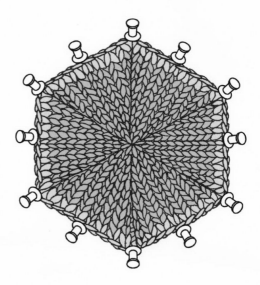

Honeycomb Purse

STEP 1. Following the instructions on page 152, make 24 hexagons with the linen yarns. Block each shape, using the template on the previous page to ensure that each one is identical in size and that the edges are all straight.

STEP 2. Refer to the assembly diagram at right for how to arrange the shapes.

STEP 3. Pin, then whipstitch (page 146) the pieces together using the same yellow yarn that edges each hexagon. (You may hide the seams by whipstitching the hexagons together with right sides facing, or let the seams show by stitching them with wrong sides together.)

THE I-CORD STRAP

STEP 1. Using size US 5 (3.75 mm) double-pointed needles and whichever of the yellow yarns you prefer, cast on 4 stitches. Do not turn the needle.

STEP 2. Slide the stitches back to the tip of the left needle. Bring the yarn behind the stitches and K4. Do not turn the needle.

STEP 3. Repeat step 2 until your I-cord is at least 24" long. Cast off, leaving an 8" tail.

STEP 4. Fold the strap in half, stitch the ends together, and securely stitch the handle in place where indicated by "X" on the assembly diagram.

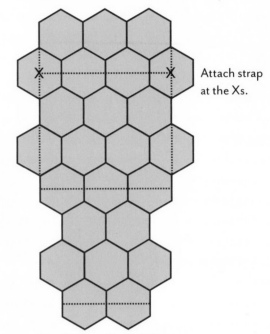

Attach strap at the Xs.

Attach pieces, then fold along dotted lines and stitch sides.

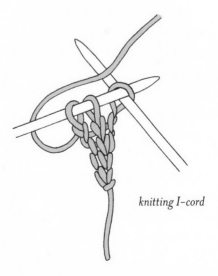

knitting I-cord

A Simple Ribbed Cowl

This ribbed cowl is worked back and forth in rows on straight needles. Suitable for knitting the *Mood Ring* (page 30) or *Walk around the Block* (page 106), this pattern uses a light worsted- or DK-weight yarn and size US 7 (4.5 mm) straight needles, for a gauge of about 5 stitches and 6 rows to an inch in the ribbed pattern. (Check the ball band on the yarn for more exact specifications.) If you knit 5 rows a day for a month with that gauge, your cowl will have a circumference of about 25". Or knit 6 rows per day for 2 months if you'd like a cowl that you wrap around your neck twice when you wear it. *Note:* You may wish to use another of your favorite stitch patterns instead of ribbing for your cowl.

SETUP

Using a US 7 (4.5 mm) needle, cast on 72 stitches. (This should give you a cowl width of about 14".)

KNITTING THE COWL

K2, P2 every row. (Notice that you'll always be knitting into knit stitches and purling into purl stitches, no matter which side of the piece you're working on.)

FINISHING

Cast off loosely, and join the two short ends of the cowl using one of the seaming methods on pages 141–143. Weave in the ends to hide them.

A Circular-Knit Cowl

This cowl is knit in rounds on circular or double-pointed needles. Suitable for knitting the cowl described for *You Are as Beautiful as the Moon* (page 66), this pattern uses a light worsted- or DK-weight yarn and a size US 7 (4.5 mm) circular needle, for a gauge of about 5 stitches and 6 rounds to an inch in your stitch pattern. (Check the ball band on the yarn for more exact specifications.)

SETUP

Using a US 7 (4.5 mm) circular needle, cast on 125 stitches. (This will give you a cowl circumference of about 25".) Use the yarn from the last cast-on stitch to knit the first cast-on stitch and begin working circularly, taking care not to twist your stitches as you do so. Place a marker between the first and last stitches, so that you can keep track of the beginning of each round.

KNITTING THE COWL

- Use any stitch pattern you prefer, but be sure to adjust the total stitch count to accommodate the stitch multiple of your chosen pattern.

- Using white yarn, knit 48 rounds (about 8").

- Using black yarn, knit another 48 rounds.

FINISHING

- Bind off.

- Bring the lengthwise edges of the cowl together, folding the cowl so that the wrong side is hidden

(continued on next page)

(A Circular-Knit Cowl, continued)

inside. Pin the edges all around, then use mattress stitch (pages 141–142) to seam the edges together.

A Scarf Knit with Short Rows

Working short rows is a way to shape your knitting by working only a section of a row, then turning before you get to the end and working all the way back to the other end, or even again working only a section and turning back. Some pattern directions include using a technique called "wrap and turn" to avoid holes at the point where you turn, but for the *Navigating by Heart* scarf (page 55), which is knit in garter stitch throughout, it's not necessary to do that.

SETUP

Decide on the scarf width you want, and cast on whatever number of stitches will provide that width using the yarn and needles you've chosen.

KNITTING THE SCARF

- Knit until you get to your first "corner," where you begin short rows. Knit 1 stitch, then turn (without knitting across the row) and knit that 1 stitch again.

- Knit 2 stitches, turn, and knit back to the beginning of the row.

- Knit 3 stitches, turn, and knit back to the beginning of the row.

- Continue in this way until you've knit all the way across the row and back.

If you want to turn the corner in another direction, follow the same procedure, but this time begin the sequence on the opposite side of the fabric. (Since in garter stitch there's no right or wrong side, you might want to put a safety pin or other marker on one side so that you'll know how to alternate the direction of the turns.)

FINISHING

When the scarf is as long as you want it, bind off. Block as described in Joining Knit Pieces Together (page 141) to secure the shape.

Man's Hourglass-Cable Tie

Designed for *Quantum Entanglement* (page 90), this tie is knit with laceweight yarn, at about 10 stitches to an inch on size US 0 (2 mm) needles. The finished width is about 2¼". You may follow the chart on this page or the written directions on the next page. If you knit the tie as a wedding gift (*A Fine Pair,* page 111), you may want to omit the cable and knit the entire tie in garter stitch.

The following abbreviations are used in this pattern:

- **T3B (TRAVELING STITCHES TO THE RIGHT):** Slip 1 stitch to a cable needle and hold in back of the work, K3 from the left needle, K1 from the cable needle.

- **T3F (TRAVELING STITCHES TO THE LEFT):** Slip 3 stitches to a cable needle and hold in front of the work, K1 from the left needle, K3 from the cable needle.

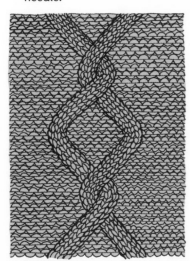

- **C6B (CABLE 6):** Slip 3 stitches to a cable needle and hold in back of the work, K3 from the left needle, K3 from the cable needle (the cable will twist to the left).

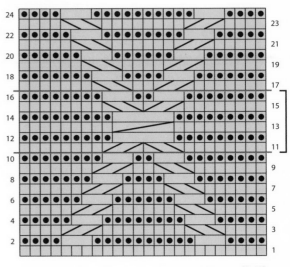

repeat rows 11–16

KEY

☐ *Knit on right side; purl on wrong side*

▣ *Purl on right side; knit on wrong side*

▱ *T3B: Slip 1 stitch to cable needle and hold in back, K3, K1 from cable needle*

▱ *T3F: Slip 3 stitches to cable needle and hold in front, K1, K3 from cable needle*

▭ *C6B (cable 6): Slip 3 stitches to cable needle and hold in back, K3, K3 from cable needle*

Odd-numbered rows are right side rows

(continued on next page)

(Man's Hourglass-Cable Tie, continued)

Cast on 24 stitches.

KNITTING THE HOURGLASS CABLE

ROW 1 (RIGHT SIDE): Knit to the end of the row.

ROW 2 (WRONG SIDE): K4, P3, K10, P3, K4.

ROW 3: K4, T3F, K8, T3B, K4.

ROW 4: K5, P3, K8, P3, K5.

ROW 5: K5, T3F, K6, T3B, K5.

ROW 6: K6, P3, K6, P3, K6.

ROW 7: K6, T3F, K4, T3B, K6.

ROW 8: K7, P3, K4, P3, K7.

ROW 9: K7, T3F, K2, T3B, K7.

ROW 10: K8, P3, K2, P3, K8.

ROW 11: K8, T3F, T3B, K8.

ROW 12: K9, P6, K9.

ROW 13: K9, C6B, K9.

ROW 14: K9, P6, K9.

ROW 15: K8, T3B, T3F, K8.

ROW 16: K8, P3, K2, P3, K8.

Repeat rows 11–16 one more time.

ROW 17: K7, T3B, K2, T3F, K7.

ROW 18: K7, P3, K4, P3, K7.

ROW 19: K6, T3B, K4, T3F, K6.

ROW 20: K6, P3, K6, P3, K6.

ROW 21: K5, T3B, K6, T3F, K5.

ROW 22: K5, P3, K8, P3, K5.

ROW 23: K4, T3B, K8, T3F, K4.

ROW 24: K4, P3, K10, P3, K4.

Repeat rows 3–24 until your tie measures 15".

KNITTING THE REST OF THE TIE

Continue to knit in garter stitch (knit every row) until the tie measures 53" long.

FINISHING

Bind off. Block as described in Joining Knit Pieces Together (page 141).

Butterfly Placemat

Each traditional Butterfly Stitch is worked over 5 stitches and 10 rows, placed on a background of plain stockinette stitch. Since the number of butterflies you knit into your placemat is the number of years you've been friends with the birthday girl, you can place them spontaneously in whatever pattern appeals to you — like real butterflies! I like to use linen yarn, or a cotton-linen blend, for placemats. They'll wash beautifully and last for years. To provide a tidy border around your placemat and also to help it lie flat, work ¾" of Seed Stitch after the cast on, then maintain 5 stitches in Seed Stitch on each side of the stockinette stitch center, and again work a ¾" border of Seed Stitch before binding off.

SETUP

For a standard 12" × 18" placemat, cast on 100 stitches of DK-weight linen yarn. Using size US 5 (3.75 mm) needles, you should get a gauge of about 5½ stitches to an inch. You may get a different gauge depending on the brand of yarn and the size needles you use, so be sure to check the label on the ball of yarn for advice, knit a swatch, and adjust the stitch count as needed.

KNITTING THE BORDER

Work Seed Stitch (see page 137) for ¾".

ADDING THE BUTTERFLIES

After the Seed Stitch border, work several rows in stockinette stitch (page 136), at the same time continuing to work 5 stitches in Seed Stitch at the beginning and end of each row for the border. When you're ready to work your first butterfly, here's how to do it, starting on a right-side row:

ROW 1 (RIGHT SIDE): Work the Seed Stitch border, then knit to the spot where you want a butterfly and slip the next 5 stitches to the right-hand needle without knitting them, keeping the working yarn in front of the needle. Knit to the border, then work Seed Stitch to the end of the row.

ROW 2: Work the border, purl across, and work the other border.

ROWS 3–8: Repeat rows 1 and 2.

ROW 9 (RIGHT SIDE): Repeat row 1.

ROW 10 (WRONG SIDE): Work the border and stockinette to where the butterfly begins, then P2, insert your right needle down through the 5 loose strands, lift the strands onto the left needle, and purl them together with the first stitch on the left needle. Complete the row in the established pattern.

FINISHING

Continue to work the borders, stockinette background, and butterflies as desired, until your placemat measures 11¼". Work a Seed Stitch top border to match the bottom border. Bind off. Block as directed on the yarn label.

IMPORTANT: In row 10, purl all stitches up to and including the stitch before the middle stitch of the 5 stitches you slipped on the knit side. After completing the row, turn your work over and

(continued on next page)

(Butterfly Placemat, continued)

notice that by purling the loose strands together with the middle stitch of the 5-stitch group, you have tacked them together right at the middle to create the symmetrical "wings" of the butterfly.

Butterfly Stitch finished

Sun Salutation Scarf

This pattern is knit using a technique called *intarsia*, which allows you to knit large sections of different colors side by side — in this case, the sun and the sky. You will need to wind two balls of the main (background) color (one can be quite small, because you will use it for only about 25 partial rows) and one ball for the sun so that you don't have to carry long strands of the main color across the back of the fabric while you're knitting the sun. You'll want your scarf to look good on both sides. The pattern also includes a knitted slit (see pages 144–145). I recommend practicing both of these techniques before the big day.

Cast on enough stitches to get the scarf width you want with the yarn and needles you are using. (See page 163 for advice about what yarn and needles to use and also refer to the information on the ball band to give you an idea of what gauge to expect. I used bulky yarn and size US 11 [8 mm] needles to get 3 stitches to an inch.) Get up a little before dawn so you can cast on and knit a few rows in the background color before the sun peeks over the horizon. I cast on 19 stitches and knit in garter stitch for 4 rows so that the bottom of the scarf wouldn't roll. I then kept 3 stitches in garter stitch along each edge for the entire length of the scarf, again to prevent the edges from rolling.

Follow the Sun Chart on the opposite page when you're ready to knit the circular sun into your scarf. There's only one trick to successfully knitting intarsia: it's important that you twist the new yarn around the old yarn each time you change to the new color. This will ensure that no holes appear where the colors meet. Here's how to do it:

STEP 1. Wind a separate ball of yarn for each color section you are working (one ball for the sun, and two balls for the "sky" — one for each section that surrounds the sun).

STEP 2. Using your sky color, knit to where you want to start the edge of the sun. Drop the sky yarn to the wrong side of the knitting, then take the sun-color yarn under and around the sky-color yarn before using it to continue knitting, thus locking the two sections of color neatly together. Follow the same procedure when you get to the other edge of the sun and need to work with the sky-color yarn again.

STEP 3. When you turn around and are knitting back to where the color sections change, each yarn that you need will be waiting for you. Again drop the yarn you have been knitting with, move it to the wrong side, and take the new yarn under and around it as you did in step 2.

STEP 4. Continue to work the 3 edge stitches on both sides in garter stitch, and stockinette stitch in the middle after you have completed the sun.

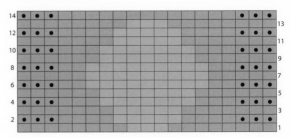

Sun Chart

1 square = 1 stitch
4 stitches = 1 inch
☐ *Knit on the right side; purl on the wrong side*
◉ *Purl on the right side; knit on the wrong side*
Odd-numbered rows are right-side rows

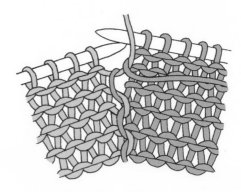

Notice how the two different yarns interlock where the new color is started.

Doodle Daydream Skirt

Begin by figuring out how many stitches to cast on for each panel of your *Doodle Daydream* skirt (page 44). The only wrong answer here is one that yields an unwearable skirt of the wrong size. To prevent such a scenario, we'll do a little math to determine how many stitches wide to make each of the six panels.

STEP 1. Using your prepared pencils and two strands of your yarn, knit a test swatch to check your gauge (that is, how many stitches you're getting per inch). Make the swatch about 20 stitches wide so that you have enough room to measure 4" in the middle.

STEP 2. Measure around your hips. Multiply your hip measurement by the number of stitches you get per inch on your swatch. (If the number of stitches per inch doesn't come out even, be sure to include the actual fraction.) Divide this total by 6, then add 2 to determine how many stitches you need per panel. (The extra 2 stitches is needed for seaming the panels together.)

STEP 3. To knit your first panel, cast the appropriate number of stitches onto one pencil and begin working your desired stitch pattern. You might want to begin all six panels with a block of matching pattern stitches. (You'll be knitting from the bottom up.) For example, on my pencil skirt, I knit the first 2" of each panel in garter stitch. This creates continuity at the bottom of the skirt after all the panels are connected, like a tidy border framing the more chaotic doodles on the rest of the skirt. Once you have your border, don't forget to doodle as you go!

STEP 4. When the panel is the length you want your skirt to be, place all the stitches on a stitch holder (or a length of scrap yarn). Now, knit five more panels.

STEP 5. Use mattress stitch (pages 141–142) to join the panels together. If you want a slit in the back, leave several inches of one of the seams unjoined.

STEP 6. Place all of the "live" stitches on a circular needle about the same diameter as your pencils or a little smaller, and knit 1 round. To create a waistband, work 2" of K1, P1 ribbing, then bind off. Turn the ribbing to the inside, matching the bound-off edge to the place where the ribbing begins. Whipstitch (page 146) this casing down, leaving an inch or so unsewn so that you can run a length of ½"-wide elastic through it. Make the elastic a length that fits your waist comfortably, run it through the casing, and then sew the ends together with needle and thread before closing the waistband opening entirely.

helpful charts

Yarn Weights, Stitch Counts, and Needle Sizes

TYPE OF YARN	NUMBER OF STITCHES IN 4"	RECOMMENDED NEEDLE SIZE	
		U.S.	**METRIC**
LACE	33–40 sts	000–1	1.5–2.25 mm
FINGERING, SOCK	27–32 sts	1–3	2.25–3.25 mm
SPORT	23–26 sts	3–5	3.25–3.75 mm
DK, LIGHT WORSTED	21–24 sts	5–7	3.75–4.5 mm
WORSTED	16–20 sts	7–9	4.5–5.5 mm
CHUNKY	12–15 sts	9–11	5.5–8 mm
BULKY	6–11 sts	11 and larger	8 mm and larger

Common Knitting Abbreviations

K	knit
k2tog	knit 2 stitches together
P	purl
p3tog	purl 3 stitches together
ssk	slip, slip, knit the 2 slipped stitches together
yo	yarnover

Standard Scarf/Shawl Sizes

SCARF

6"–10" × 65"

10"–12" × 70"

SHAWL

28"–36" × 80"

Standard Throw/Blanket Sizes

INFANT RECEIVING BLANKET

23", 24", or 36" square

29" × 32"

30" × 36"

STROLLER OR CARRIAGE BLANKET

30" × 40"

CRIB BLANKET

28" × 42"

30" × 40"

36" × 42"

36" × 46"

THROW/AFGHAN

48" × 60"

50" × 70"

Uncommon Abbreviations

BO	be open-minded
dec	decrease stress
inc	increase courage
K	know by heart
k2tog	knit 2 places together
M1	make someone's day
P	play like a child
psso	pass sweet stitches over
pwise	pearls of wisdom
rep	repeat as many times as it brings you joy
RS	right side of the bed
sk	skip through autumn leaves
ss	slip off to sleep
St st	starry stitch
tog	side by side, hand in hand
WS	welcome spontaneity
wyib	with yarn in the berry patch
wyif	with yarn in the flowers
yo	yarn over the moon

index

acknowledgments

My very thoughtful editor asked me where the idea for knitting the sky came from. I'm honestly not sure where this all started, but her question sparked a memory for me. A decade ago, a dear old friend and I took a road trip to the Oregon coast. We composed haikus together as we drove through a place near and dear to both of our hearts. Side by side, we witnessed the landscape scrolling by — tall pines, low ferns, covered bridges, and roadside chainsaw sculptures. When the clouds caught our attention, we wrote the following haiku:

Clouds caught in treetops.
Branches carding wisps of wool.
Spinning memories.

Only years later did it occur to me to turn this poetic snippet into a tangible form that I could swing around my neck. The idea seemed to come out of thin air — a pure free gift — but of course that can't be the full story. To what or whom can I give thanks for this way of knitting, this way of seeing and being, I have come to hold so dear?

Is it because my mother was a Montessori preschool teacher? Perhaps it was the berry picking with my grandmother. Or maybe it was snorkeling through towers of kelp as a child? Was it that one extraordinary philosophy professor, the one who talked about the spaces *in between* things? What about my friend with the sheep farm — the one who taught me to spin? Or the fact that I spent a summer back in college researching the history of sheep and wool in the Pacific Northwest? Oh! It could be that gorgeous passage from my favorite book, *Pilgrim at Tinker Creek,* in which infinite life on earth appears in a dream in the shape of a woman's tweed scarf, a scarf with no beginning and no end. And then there's my brilliant friend who did an art project in which she walked a mile in other people's shoes — literally. Or what about my other dear friend, the one who sings, who always welcomes my strange ideas and gives me her phenomenal two cents? Oh, and I have another lovely friend who designs beautiful meals based on personal stories.

In the end, it was and continues to be all these people, places, things, and more that make this book, this way of seeing and being, possible. I carry infinite gratitude for having crossed paths with these creative companions over the years and I look forward to what's ahead.

special thanks

Thank you to Storey Publishing for corralling my wild ideas into the tidy object that is this book. To my editor, Gwen Steege: you have been an absolute delight. I am grateful for your vision, encouragement, warm heart, and technical expertise. To Alethea Morrison: thank you for making it beautiful. To Lauren Nassef: it's such a treat to have your paintbrush grace these pages. Lastly, thank you to my sweet brother for all sorts of help along the way.

about the author

LEA REDMOND is always looking for the poem hiding inside of things: a salt shaker, a clothes tag, a hand gesture, a cloud. Forever fascinated by the way experiences can slip from the ordinary to the extraordinary, she endeavors to make things that hold this possibility. Explore her whimsical world and participate in creative projects at LeaRedmond.com. Also visit her online shop at LeafcutterDesigns.com, where you can send a "world's smallest letter" and order other playful goods.

knitthesky.com

For additional creative patterns, yarn kits, and other bonus materials, join thousands of adventurous knitters online at KnitTheSky.com. Share your work, discover inspiring new ideas, and improve your skills with our tips and tutorial videos.

You'll also find vibrant Knit the Sky communities on: Ravelry.com — *ravelry.com/groups/knit-the-sky* Instagram — *#knitthesky*

about the illustrator

LAUREN NASSEF is an illustrator and artist living in Chicago. She graduated with a BFA in Painting from The Rhode Island School of Design in 2001.